MAXIMILIAN I

ROBERT SETON-WATSON

Published 2017 by Didactic Press

CONTENTS

I

THERE is a peculiar difficulty in bridging over long periods of history, and in clearing our minds of the habits and prejudices of today, before we criticize characters and events which belong to distant periods and other lands. This difficulty, in spite of the strange charm which encourages us to surmount it, makes itself all the more felt in a Transition Period, such as the close of the fifteenth, and the dawn of the sixteenth century. The breath of new ideas is in the air.

"The old order changed, yielding place to new", but the old dreams are not yet banished from the imagination, and the old ideals have not yet wholly lost their power. Change is everywhere apparent, consummation is still a dream of the far-distant future. To those who look for a figure typical of the age, Maximilian stands forth pre-eminent. Heir to all the splendid traditions of the Caesars and the later glories of the Saxon and Franconian Emperors, he filled the highest position of

Germany, not in an attitude of indifference or aloofness, but devoting all his energies and sympathies to every movement or aspiration of his time. His actual achievements in the hard concrete of facts are, from a national point of view, but small; but these are more than balanced by his activity in other and more abstract directions. It is in his relations to the budding thought of modern life that we can feel the real charm and fascination of Maximilian's character. For his was a nature which could never rest satisfied with the past, and aspired to ends which only the far distant future was destined to attain.

Maximilian cannot fairly be judged solely from an historical standpoint; from this a judgment in the main unfavorable would be difficult to avoid. For his task was to bridge over a necessary period of transition—to check the perils of innovation, to employ political expedients which could not, from their very nature, stand the shock of later developments, and to make shift with materials and resources which were soon to be altered or replaced. Hence his achievements, though of very real value to his own age, have left but few traces visible to modern eyes. The Southern temperament which he inherited from his mother often drove him into foolhardy adventures, from which he only extricated himself with a loss of dignity. But the questionable results of his headlong enthusiasms are atoned for by the noble ideals which prompted them; and the very traits which were disastrous to his political career have earned for him his truest claims to greatness.

To tell the life-story of an idealist seems to be repugnant to the most modern of historical methods. Hard dry facts must be summoned to describe his career; an array of political exploits and the wearisome details of fruitless legal reforms must be poured forth in profitless and unending monotony. The soul and its impulses, human or divine, seem no monger to be admitted to the chamber of the historian, whose dull and regulated pulse scorns to beat faster at the tragedy of human lives. But if there is one case in which a true account must not be limited to mere facts, it is that of Maximilian. The specious system of accumulating details, coldly balancing them, and leaving the reader to judge, would be utterly unfair in his case. As well attempt to do justice to Luther, while omitting the agonies and self-reproach of his cloister life, the deep formative influence of those silent months upon the Wartburg, as estimate Maximilian, the dreamer and idealist, by the necessities of his purse or the extravagance of his vast designs! His personality and his office do not by any means coincide. There are many features of his character which have no connection with the government of his lands, which the historians of his own day overlooked, and which would still be overlooked from a strictly political and historical point of view. But while our admiration is aroused by his active share in the great living movements of the age, it must be confessed that his versatility and breadth of interest have an unfortunate counterpart in the fickleness and lack of concentration which led him to flit from scheme to scheme, without ever allowing any single one to attain to maturity. Such inconstancy in a sovereign is usually negatived, or at least held in bounds, by the apparatus of government. But in this case all centred in Maximilian himself, and not even the influential Matthew Lang was entirely trusted in high affairs of state. As a rule, Maximilian could not endure to have men of masterly or original character about him, mainly owing to the passionate conviction with which he clung to his own opinions, and partly perhaps to a half-conscious fear of unfavorable comparisons. We are thus driven to the conclusion that his policy is mainly his own work, and that, though inspired by lofty patriotism and definite family and territorial ambitions, he never succeeded in combining the two motives, and finally left the problem unsolved and insoluble. But this conviction should only serve to remind us that his greatest achievements lie outside the province of politics. Indeed, regarded as a whole, his life is not so much a great historical drama, as an epic poem of chivalry, rich in bright colors and romantic episodes, and crowded with the swift turns and surprises of fortune.

II

TO describe the events of Maximilian's political career with any sort of detail would be to narrate the history of Europe during one of its most fascinating and complicated phases. To an essay such as the present such a scheme must be entirely alien; and for its purposes Maximilian's life may be broadly divided into two periods. In the first, which ends with 1490, his ambitions are directed towards the West; and Burgundy, the Netherlands, and the French frontier claim his whole attention. But in the midst of his designs against France, new developments at home summon him away. The acquisition of Tyrol and the recovery of Austria shift the centre of gravity from West to East, and his accession to the Empire finally compels him to take up new threads of policy, which point him to the East and the South rather than to the West. In this later period, which is more purely political, and in which the character of Maximilian is perhaps less marked, the main trend of his policy is towards the re-establishment of Imperial influence in Italy, and combinations either against the French or the Turks. In each case he is doomed to disappointment; and the misfortunes that arise from his continual lack of money and resources form a story at once irritating and pathetic.

While engaged in certain operations against the County of Cilly, 1452, the Emperor Frederick III narrowly escaped capture by the enemy. He ascribed his safety to a dream, in which St. Maximilian warned him of his danger; and thus when his wife presented him with a son, the infant received the name of his father's saintly patron.

Maximilian was born at Neustadt near Vienna on May 22, 1459. His mother, Eleanor of Portugal, whose marriage to Frederick III has been immortalized by theabrush of Pinturicchio, was a princess of lively wit and considerable talent: and many points of his character are to be traced to the Southern temperament of Eleanor, rather than to the phlegmatic and ineffectual nature of Frederick.

His early years were times of stress and trouble; and, while still an infant, he shared the dangers of his parents, who were closely besieged in the citadel of Vienna by Albert of Austria and the insurgent citizens. To such straits was the slender garrison reduced, that the young prince is said to have wandered through the castle vaults, tearfully begging the servants for a piece of bread. In spite of a vigorous defense, Frederick must have yielded to superior force, but for the timely assistance of his allies, the Bohemians, through whose influence peace was restored between the rival brothers. The death of Albert in 1463 left Frederick supreme in Austria and its dependencies. But his past experiences had inspired him with a very natural prejudice against the citizens of Vienna; and they, on their part, were never slow to reveal the dislike and contempt in which they held their Imperial master. This mutual ill-feeling largely accounts for the ease with which Matthias effected the conquest of Austria. Frederick, at first from choice, later from necessity, chose Linz or Graz as his Austrian residences, and never overcame his distrust of the Viennese.

Thus it was that Maximilian's childhood was spent at Wiener Neustadt, thirteen miles S.E. from Vienna. His education was entrusted to Peter Engelbrecht, afterwards Bishop of Wiener Neustadt; and we learn that up to the age of six he found great difficulty in articulating. This may have thrown him back somewhat; and, indeed, he himself complained in later days of his bad education. "If Peter, my teacher, still lived" he declared, "I would make him live near me, in order to teach him how to bring up children". But Maximilian's strictures are probably undeserved, and may be due to the fact that his tutor restrained him from the study of history, which he loved, and held him down to Latin and dialectics, even enforcing them upon his unwilling pupil by rudely practical methods. Certainly, if we may judge by the accounts furnished in Weisskunig, which seems the most reliable of the books compiled under Maximilian's supervision, there were but few pursuits, physical or mental, in which the young Prince had not his share. Not merely was he instructed in the art of war, and in the technical details of various trades, such as carpentry and founding, but also in the prevailing theories of statesmanship and government. These are quaintly divided by the young White King under five heads—the all-mightiness of God, the influence of the planets on Man's destiny, the reason of Man, excessive mildness in administration, and excessive severity in power; and his discourse on the subject wins the complete approval of his father and the wonder of his biographer. Everything which Maximilian does approaches perfection; if he fishes, he catches more than other men; he cures horses of which all the horse-doctors have despaired; he has few equals as blacksmith or locksmith. But though all this is clearly exaggeration, it yet affords a clue to the accomplishments to which Maximilian was brought up, and to the many sidedness of his early training. There is no doubt as to his proficiency as a linguist; he could speak Latin, French,

13

Italian and Flemish fluently, and had some knowledge of Spanish, Walloon, and English besides. His thirst for knowledge was almost unquenchable, and increased with his years—history, mathematics, languages, all receiving attention from the Royal student. But his literary tastes, even in later life, never superseded his love of manly exercises; and it was no doubt in his early years that he first acquired that passion for the chase which never deserted him. His marvellous adventures in pursuit of the chamois or the bear are still remembered in the Tyrolese Alps.

He possessed the most dauntless courage, and is said to have been one of the finest swordsmen in Europe. He had few equals at the tourney; and one of the most romantic incidents of his life was the single combat at Worms, when, entering the lists in the simplest of armour, he overcame a famous French knight, and then, raising his vizor, revealed his identity amid the deafening plaudits of the crowd. Nor were his exploits confined to chivalrous amusements : time and again he proved his courage on the field of battle; notably at Guinegate, where "he raged like a lion in the fight", and later, with characteristic generosity, devoted himself to dressing the wounds of the vanquished. Gallant, chivalrous and versatile, full of high ideals and noble enthusiasms, he was formed by nature to be the darling of his age and nation.

Such general characteristics must suffice for a description of Maximilian's early life, of which we possess but few details or facts, until the Burgundian marriage brought him into the full blaze of the political arena. This famous event, whose results are still to be traced in the political conditions of Europe, was the first step of the House of Hapsburg towards the "Weltmacht" of Charles V.

To Frederick III belongs the credit of this achievement. During his long reign of fifty-three years the Imperial crown lost much of its remaining prestige and influence; and it is undoubtedly true that Frederick used his Imperial office for purposes of Hapsburg aggrandizement. But he can hardly be blamed for adopting a policy to which there was no alternative. Chosen mainly for his impotence, he had literally no hold upon the Empire itself, beyond the largely nominal prerogatives of his office; and he had good precedent for his scheme of attaining to real Imperial power by building up a compact territorial state. Something must be allowed to a prince who, with such slight resources as Frederick III, could aspire to the proud motto, "Alles Erdreich ist Oesterreich Unterthan", and who, after years of disaster and disappointment, succeeded in laying the foundations of a greatness which he did not live to see. The policy of the Hohenstauffen was no longer practicable. The power of the Emperor had all but vanished, and the sole way of meeting the territorial tendencies of the great princes was to develop a territorial power for himself. The task required a man of courage and endurance, who should paralyze the opposing forces by passive resistance; and such a man was Frederick. That the Burgundian marriage was no mere lucky accident, but the fruit of a long and deliberate policy, is abundantly shown by the negotiations which preceded the event. A life-long struggle against inadequate means effectually soured the character of the old monarch, but it had not been wholly in vain; and the marked contrast between father and son may perhaps account for the unfavourable light in which Frederick has been viewed by posterity.

The first suggestion of a marriage between Maximilian and Mary of Burgundy occurs in a letter of Pius II to Philip the Good in 1463. The Pope doubtless hoped that an alliance of Austria and Burgundy would further his great scheme of a crusade against the Turks; but even hints of a kingly title failed to rouse the old Duke's interest in the proposal, and it seems to have been allowed to drop. In 1468 an envoy appeared at the Burgundian Court, with full powers to treat as to the marriage, and the election of Charles the Bold as King of the Romans. But the latter's soaring ambitions were a hindrance to the marriage; and when the long negotiations for the revival of the old Burgundian kingdom came to nothing in 1474, Frederick's object seemed as far from fulfillment as ever. Throughout Charles's reign there was a continual danger of the prize falling to some more favored suitor. It was only when the Burgundian arms first met with disaster at the hands of the Swiss, that Charles's day dreams began to be dispelled, and he gave serious thought to the future of his only child. A month after the defeat of Grandson, an Imperial embassy waited upon the Duke; and on May 6, 1476, the betrothal of Maximilian and Mary was formally announced. In its immediate results, the alliance was disastrous to Charles; for his desertion by the Prince of Taranto, one of Mary's disappointed suitors, the day before the battle of Morat, was one of the causes of his second defeat by the Swiss. Charles now became anxious to hasten on the marriage, and sent an envoy to obtain his daughter's consent. On November 4, he wrote to Frederick begging him and Maximilian to come with all speed to Köln for the ceremony; and soon after, Maximilian received a letter from his bride, thanking him for the letter and ring which he had sent her, and declaring her agreement with her father. But now, as ever, Frederick was tied down by want of money, and the final catastrophe, when Charles the Bold perished on the field of Nancy (January 6, 1477), found the bridegroom quite unprepared for his new and arduous task. At a time when so much depended on prompt action, the Emperor contented himself with sending despatches to the officials and stadtholders of the Low Countries, urging them to obey none but Mary and Maximilian as her betrothed husband, and promising to come in person at the earliest possible date. Meanwhile, Mary's position was pitiable in the extreme. The ungallant citizens of Ghent took prompt advantage of her weakness by extorting from her "The Great Privilege" : the chief cities refused to pay taxes; and French agents everywhere incited the burghers to rebellion.

Louis XI did not imitate his cousin of Austria, and lost no time in profiting by Mary's helpless condition. In the course of a few weeks, Picardy, Franche Comté, and the Duchy of Burgundy were annexed to the French Crown. King Louis demanded, almost at the sword's point, the hand of Mary for the infant Dauphin; and his ungenerous betrayal of her secret overtures exposed her to an unpardonable affront at the hands of her disloyal subjects. Despite her tears and entreaties, and before her very eyes, her two most trusted counsellors were executed by the citizens of Ghent; and the young Duchess found herself friendless and alone, at the mercy of the treacherous Louis and her own rebellious people. In her distress she turned naturally to her knight and protector, Maximilian, whose admirers pictured to her a new Lohengrin destined at the last moment to restore the desperate fortunes of Elsa of Brabant. The romance of this journey to succour his Princess in distress is somewhat marred by the long delay which preceded it. It can only be explained by the money difficulties of his father, and the intrigues of Matthias of Hungary, which brought him to the verge of war with

Frederick. Notwithstanding Mary's pressing entreaties for his coming, it was only on May 21 that Maximilian left Vienna, and he did not actually reach Ghent till August 18. But though this delay was of great advantage to Louis XI, it may be doubted whether Maximilian could have effected much, even had he arrived on the scene at an earlier date. The Ghentois were probably hostile to him, or sank their opposition mainly because of the distance of his own dominions. It was the growing fear of French predominance which won adherents to his cause, and he found many supporters among the Flemish nobles, and the party of the Hoeks. The old Netherland chronicler gives us a favourable sketch of Maximilian, when he says: "Though still a youth, he displayed the true qualities of a man and a prince. He was magnanimous, brave and liberal, born for the good of the race. His fame was increased by a countenance of right royal dignity, the splendour of his father's majesty, the antiquity of his lineage, and the amplitude of his inheritance". The day after his arrival in Ghent, the marriage was celebrated by the Legate with great pomp and rejoicings.

"I beheld the pageants splendid, that adorned those days of old;

Stately dames, like queens attended, knights who bore the fleece of gold;

Lombard and Venetian merchants with deep-laden argosies;

Ministers from twenty nations; more than royal pomp and ease.

I beheld proud Maximilian, kneeling humbly on the ground;

I beheld the gentle Mary, hunting with her hawk and hound".

The young Prince seems at first to have carried all before him; and as we read the words of an eyewitness of the proceedings, our charmed fancy pictures for us one of the deathless paladins of Charles the Great. "Mounted on a large chestnut horse, clad in silver armour, his head uncovered, his flowing locks bound with a circlet of pearls and precious stones, Maximilian looks so glorious in his youth, so strong in his manliness, that I know not which to admire most—the beauty of his youth, the bravery of his manhood, or the promise of his future". From the very first the marriage seems to have been one of great happiness; and the birth of Philip (June 1478) set a crown to their affection. Maximilian himself gives a happy description of his wife in a confidential letter to Sigismund Prüschenk: "I have a lovely good virtuous wife ... She is small of body, much smaller than 'die Rosina', and snow-white. Brown hair, a small nose, a small head and features, brown and grey eyes mixed, clear and beautiful. Her mouth is somewhat high, but pure and red". Mary was a fine horsewoman, and excelled at most forms of sport; and this formed an additional link between them. "My wife is thoroughly at home with falcons and hounds; she has a greyhound of great pace".

In all affairs of Government Mary yielded to her husband, and they remained in complete accord till the day of her death. On Maximilian devolved the task of repelling the French attacks, and we find him complaining of the stress of business which filled every moment of the day.

Infusing his own vigour into his new subjects, and substantially aided by the Imperial Diet, he was ere long enabled to take the offensive; and on August 7, 1478, gained a complete victory over the French at Guinegate. The personal prowess which Maximilian displayed, while it helps to explain the estimation in which he was held, inevitably suggests that he was more brilliant as a soldier than as a commander. For so decisive a success, the results were remarkably small. Maximilian's sanguine nature induced him to reject Louis' overtures for peace, and though the tide of invasion had been rolled back, the most favourable time for a satisfactory settlement was allowed to pass. But while Maximilian eagerly awaited the death of the French King, he was himself plunged into mourning and disaster by the sudden death of Mary (March 27, 1482). Filled with the liveliest grief at his unexpected bereavement, he found that at the same time he had lost control of the source of his authority; and though recognized by Brabant and Holland, he met with nothing but opposition from the refractory Flemings. Louis XI could not repress his delight at the welcome news, and confided to the sagacious Comines his hopes of Maximilian's discomfiture. Nor was he mistaken in his forecast of events. Without even consulting Maximilian, the Flemings ratified the Treaty of Arras with Louis XI. By it the guardianship of Philip was entrusted to the Estates of Flanders; and the infant Margaret was to be educated at the French Court as the bride of the Dauphin Charles. Artois and Franche Comté, over which the Flemings had not the slightest legal control, were calmly ceded as her immediate dowry. To this humiliating treaty Maximilian had perforce to give his assent, and it was not till 1485 that the Flemings recognized him as the guardian of his son. Even then his authority was hedged in by various conditions; and the young Duke might not be removed from the country. Maximilian continued to reside in the Netherlands; but the favour which he bestowed on his own countrymen, as well as his influence in Brabant and Holland, soon rekindled the jealousy of the Flemings, who accused him of prolonging the war against France for his own private ends. He could not leave the Low Countries without ruining his position and prospects, and abandoning his children to the mercy of the Ghent citizens; French agents were ready to make the most of even a temporary absence; and he was powerless to assist his father in his unequal struggle with Matthias. But even want of money or resources does not excuse the indifference with which he treated the news of Frederick's misfortunes. The old Emperor was driven from his capital, the whole of Lower Austria fell into the hands of Matthias, and it was only the remonstrances of Venice which assured to Frederick his Adriatic provinces. There was an evident coolness at this period between father and son, and this was not removed by Maximilian's dealings with the Electors, in the hope of securing his election as King of the Romans.

Frederick had been chosen Emperor mainly for his insignificance, but it was felt that he had played the part of a nonentity only too well. There was a growing inclination to turn from Frederick to Maximilian, and to shift the duties of the Empire's struggle with Matthias of Hungary on to the Burgundian possessions of the Hapsburg House. Various causes combined to secure Maximilian's election: but none of the credit can be assigned to Frederick III, who only consented to entertain the idea, when he had become a fugitive from his dominions, and when Maximilian had promised not to make inroads upon his Imperial power. Frederick's manifest dislike of the scheme was a recommendation with most of the Electors. Maximilian was welcomed by Albert Achilles and the old Imperial party, who wished a strong ruler at the head of the

Empire; and his favourable attitude towards Reform won favour with the party of Berthold of Henneberg, the great Elector of Mainz. The opposition of France and Hungary was met by the secrecy of the Electors; and their choice was announced almost before the suspicions of Uladislas had been aroused (February 16, 1486). Frederick is said to have wept feebly at the news, but elsewhere the announcement gave rise to the most sanguine anticipations; and the gorgeous ceremonial of his coronation at Aachen made a sensible impression upon the popular mind. The proclamation of a ten years' Landfriede throughout the Empire, which was the new King's first act, was perhaps better calculated to please the Reforming party than the rank of the knights, whose brightest ornament Maximilian was held to be; yet it seemed to augur well for a new era of peace and order.

In 1488 a new instrument was devised for the enforcement of the Landfriede. The private feuds, so frequent and so ruinous in mediaeval times, were now falling into disuse, but only because the general unrest took larger forms. Leagues and Unions superseded the looser ties of warlike neighbours, and whole districts became involved in the settlement of some contemptible quarrel. The Swiss Confederacy was in reality a development of this system of Leagues, its primary object being protection against the House of Hapsburg. Every access of strength on the part of the Swiss, and especially the prestige which their triumph over Charles the Bold had won them, tended to weaken the Hapsburg influence in Swabia, the cradle of their race, and their mainstay in the Empire. Thus, when in 1486 the Bavarian Dukes directly infringed the Landfriede by their seizure of Regensburg, the moment seemed favourable for some fresh organization, which should preserve the peace of the Empire and at the same time restore the waning Hapsburg power in Swabia. In July 1487 an invitation was issued in the name of Frederick and Maximilian to all the nobles, knights, prelates and cities of Swabia, to a meeting at Esslingen. This step resulted in the formation of the famous Swabian League. Though really a development of the League of St. George's Shield, whose captain, Count Hugo von Werdenberg, was the chief originator of the scheme, it differed from it by extending its membership from the ranks of the nobles of all orders and classes of the Empire. A confederate Council and Court of Justice were instituted, and expenses were allotted for the raising of an army of 12,000 foot and 1,200 horse. A decisive influence was preserved to the Emperor, and the League was further strengthened by the adhesion of such princes as Sigismund of Tyrol, Eberhard ofWurtemberg, and the Electors of Mainz and Trier. The Swabian League remained for many years a leading factor in German affairs. Though it widened the gulf between the Swiss and the members of the Empire (and thus no doubt was partly responsible for the Swiss war of ten years later), it also checked the gradual drifting of single towns from the Imperial to the Swiss system. And still more, it gave the Hapsburgs a strong weapon of defence against the House of Wittelsbach, whose aggressive policy might, without it, have proved entirely successful.

Meanwhile, so far from Maximilian realizing the hopes of the Electors by bringing the forces of the Netherlands to the aid of the Empire, it was not very long ere Imperial troops were needed to rescue him from the hands of his turbulent subjects. He was rapidly becoming unpopular among the Netherlands, whose constitutional traditions were vitally opposed to his dynastic plans; and the French Government, strong in Flemish sympathy, renewed the war with greater vigour and success. Maximilian's first organized body of landsknechts was completely defeated at Bethune, and afterwards roughly handled by their nominal allies.

The final outbreak was largely due to a commercial treaty between Maximilian and Henry VII, which closed the Flemish harbours to English products. As a result, a lively commercial intercourse in English cloth sprang up in the coast towns of Brabant, and the economic rivals of Flanders reaped a rich harvest. The French Government fanned the flame of Flemish disaffection. It declared Maximilian to have forfeited the French fief of Flanders, and formally absolved this country from all allegiance to him. His refusal to account for the expenditure of the public money was an additional grievance; and when a rash visit to Bruges, with but a slender escort of troops, placed him in their power, the burghers used their advantage to the full. The morning after his entry a sudden insurrection took place (February 10, 1488). The whole town was soon up in arms, the gates were seized, and the Ducal palace was stormed by an excited mob. Maximilian himself was removed to the Kranenburg, and closely guarded; his councillors were racked in the public square, some of his chief adherents were beheaded, and the citizens of Ghent and Bruges united in depriving him of the Regency, and forming a new government wholly subservient to France. For three months he remained in this perilous condition, in continual fear of death or betrayal to Charles VIII.

Kunz von der Rosen, his faithful jester, who shared his captivity, begged Maximilian to exchange clothes with him and thus escape from the city in disguise; but the latter refused to expose him to almost certain death at the hands of the infuriated mob. Maximilian's letter to his father and the Electors shows the imminent danger in which he lay. "They will give me poison to eat, and so kill me ... they are taking all my people from me; this is my last letter for good and all ... I beseech you, in the name of God and Justice, for counsel and aid". For once Frederick's sluggish nature was fully roused, and, relinquishing all other objects, he moved heaven and earth to obtain his son's release. Over 20,000 men answered to the Imperial summons to Köln, and by the middle of May this army was advancing on Liège. The news of its approach brought the rebels to reason, and led them to hasten on negotiations with Maximilian. Without awaiting the liberating army, he gave his consent to the most humiliating terms, and solemnly pledged himself not to repudiate the agreement. By it he was to win the consent of the Emperor and Electors, and to withdraw all foreign troops from the Netherlands within eight days. He renounced, for Flanders, the guardianship of Philip, and acceded to. the formation of a Council of Regency and to a peace with France (May 16). On the strength of these promises he was liberated, and joined his father's army at Liège. Frederick and the Princes refused to recognize any such agreement; it was declared invalid and contrary to his coronation oath, on the ground that the Flemings were subjects of the Empire; and Maximilian, weakly yielding to their pressure, contented himself with returning the 55,000 groschen which had been granted him to lessen the bitterness of the pill. The march was resumed, and Ghent was closely invested. But as usual the old Emperor effected little or nothing, the town made a vigorous defence, and Maximilian was glad to avail himself of events in Germany, which claimed his attention. It is useless to attempt to justify his repudiation of his oath, for he had carefully precluded himself from all lawful methods of evasion. It leaves a deep stain upon his honour, and the most that can be said for him is that it is the one indefensible action of his life.

After an absence of twelve years Maximilian returned to the Empire in December 1488, leaving Duke Albert of Saxony as his representative in the Netherlands. The latter showed his zeal by his promise "so to serve his master that men should write of it for 1,000 years", and displayed great ability both as a commander and an organizer. The cause of peace was furthered by the Treaty of Frankfort (July 7, 1489), in accordance with which Charles VIII was to use his influence with the Flemings, and an interview was to be arranged between him and Maximilian for the settlement of the Burgundian question. As a result of this treaty, Flanders again recognized Maximilian as lawful Regent and guardian of his son, and granted him the sum of 300,000 gold thalers in token of their submission.

The readiness with which Charles VIII concluded peace was due to the recent turn of affairs in Brittany, to which country his rivalry with Maximilian was now transferred. During the aggressive war waged by France in the Netherlands the King of the Romans had found a natural ally in the Duke of Brittany, who dreaded the expansive policy of the French King. The death of Francis II (September, 1488) left the Breton throne to his young daughter Anne; and Ferdinand V and Henry VII united to protect her against her dangerous neighbour. But this protection was on the whole rather sympathetic than practical; and the insecurity of her position led the young Duchess to search the political horizon for some efficient defender. She turned to Maximilian as the sovereign most interested in resistance to France and most likely to afford her practical aid. It seemed as though the romantic episode of his first marriage was to be re-enacted in a new quarter. On March 20, 1490, Anne and Maximilian were betrothed, and towards the end of the year the marriage was formally celebrated by proxy. Anne openly assumed the title of Queen of the Romans, and Maximilian's diplomacy was for the time triumphant. But the acquisition of Brittany was a matter of supreme importance to the French Crown; and Charles VIII strained every nerve to secure the discomfiture of his rival. Brittany was overrun by French troops, Nantes surrendered after a feeble resistance, and Anne found herself closely besieged in Rennes, with little prospect of timely relief, and with a strong French faction within the walls. Maximilian's hands were tied down by the necessities of the Hungarian war, and, confident in the validity of his union with Anne, and relying on the promised aid of Henry VII, he stirred not a muscle in her defence. At last Anne found herself forced to come to terms. Brittany was to remain in the hands of the French, and free passage was granted to her through French territory, on her way to join Maximilian. But her feeling as a Princess overcame her feeling as a woman. She was naturally reluctant to leave her ancestral dominions in hostile hands for the sake of a man whom she had never seen and who was her senior by seventeen years; and her offended pride at Maximilian's inexcusable absence at her time of need led her footsteps to Chateau Langeais rather than to the German frontier. The cunning Charles had all prepared, and was able to produce the double dispensation of Innocent VIII. On December 6, 1491, the marriage of Charles VIII and Anne of Brittany was duly solemnized at Langeais, and Brittany was finally incorporated with France.

Maximilian, mainly owing to his dilatory conduct, thus found himself exposed to the most unpardonable of insults at the hands of a mere stripling. Not merely had Charles VIII deprived him of his lawful wife and her inheritance, but in so doing he repudiated Maximilian's daughter Margaret, who, since 1482, had been educated at the Court of Charles as the future Queen of France. To aggravate matters, Charles showed no inclination to restore Margaret's magnificent dowry, which consisted of Artois, Picardy and Franche Comté. Nothing could exceed Maximilian's indignation, and, full of threats of vengeance, he entered into an offensive alliance against France with the Kings of England and Spain.

But the acquisition of Brittany had set a seal to the internal consolidation of France, and Charles, having deprived his enemies of an excellent base for hostile operations, was now free to indulge in his golden dreams of foreign conquest. No concession was thought too great to secure the neutrality of his neighbours. Henry VII was bought off by hard cash and by the promise of a yearly pension; Ferdinand was appeased by the cession of the coveted provinces of Roussillon and Cerdagne. Maximilian, whose troops were meeting with some success in Franche Comté, saw himself deserted by his allies, and consented to pocket his outraged dignity in return for the substantial concessions of the Peace of Senlis (May 23, 1493). His daughter Margaret was restored, and the French evacuated Franche Comté, Artois and Nevers, in favour of the young Archduke Philip.

III

WITH the Breton incident we reach the close of Maximilian's Western career, and are free to examine the events which engaged his attention while Charles VIII was robbing him of his bride. The exigences of Hapsburg policy and of his imperial office now draw him into all the various currents of European diplomacy, and it is hardly to be wondered at, if his personality is sometimes lost sight of in an attempt to connect the intricate threads of contemporary politics. Maximilian the man and the chevalier must be our subject, rather than Maximilian the politician. The kaleidoscope of political combinations must be left to a Sismondi or a Creighton. For it is from the description of his earlier years and of his later relations to Humanism and Art that we gain the truest insight into the charm and fascination of his character—the romantic incidents which made the nation mourn him as the Last of the Knights, and the versatility which dazzled the eyes of so many brilliant contemporaries.

On his return to the Empire, Maximilian found that his presence was urgently needed in Tyrol, where Duke Sigismund, after a long reign of folly and mismanagement, could hardly restrain the general discontent in his dominions from open expression. The incapable old Duke had in later life fallen completely under the power of his mistresses, who played upon his superstitions by incantations and witch-processes, and who squandered the revenues on their own worthless ends. His life-long hatred of Frederick III, which even the cession of Vorder-Austria (1463) could not remove, filled him with the idea that his cousins wished to deprive him during his lifetime, and inclined him towards the Bavarian Court, which eagerly furthered the misunderstanding. The sale of Burgau(1486) to Duke George the Rich called attention to the possibility of Sigismund leaving his possessions outside the Hapsburg family. Bavaria was again responsible for Sigismund's war with Venice; and when defeat came and money failed, the Duke was obliged to sell all the Vorder-Austria lands to Dukes Albert and George on terms which made recovery doubtful. The Austrian party in Tyrol now insisted upon the summons of a Diet, and the Estates subjected Sigismund to an "Ordnung", by which, in return for the payment of his debts, he was restricted to a limited expenditure every year. In the event of his violation of this Ordnung, the Estates were at liberty to choose another Prince from the House of Austria. The Dukes of Bavaria had been brought to reason by the formation of the Swabian League, and raised no serious opposition to this blighting of their hopes. As was to be expected, six months had not elapsed ere Sigismund had broken through the Ordnung; while Albert of Bavaria put in a demand for 100,000 florins, in recompense for the sinking of his claims. This development brought the old Emperor to Innsbruck, whither he was followed in April 1489 by Maximilian. The latter, who entertained more friendly feelings than his father towards Bavaria, maintained a mediatory position. At last, on March 16, 1490, the long-desired step was taken. Sigismund made a formal renunciation of Tyrol, and all his other dominions in favour of Maximilian, contenting himself with a fixed income and free rights of hunting and fishing. Almost at the same time Maximilian was recognized heir by Count Bernard of Gorz.

But by that irony of fate which pursued him throughout life, Maximilian was never permitted to finish any one thing thoroughly. Time and again we see him ruined by an excess of alternatives, and by his inability to devote himself exclusively to one out of many objects.

Less than a month after Sigismund's abdication, the death of Matthias Corvinus diverted Maximilian's attention to those ancestral dominions from which his father had been so ignominiously expelled, and justified him in the hope of restoring the old Hapsburg influence over Hungary. Frederick's claim to the latter kingdom was based on the agreement of 1463, ratified by Matthias and the leading Magyar nobles, by which Frederick or his son was to succeed, if Matthias should die childless. Though this condition was now fulfilled, the Hungarians were by no means disposed to act upon it; and Vladislas, King of Bohemia, was a dangerous rival to the Hapsburgs, both by reason of the nearness of his dominions and the strength of his hereditary claims. Several causes combined to handicap Maximilian. His father, with his usual jealousy, refused to waive his rights in favour of Maximilian, who alone was capable of carrying the enterprise to a successful issue. Want of money, his curse throughout life, told heavily against him; nor was any assistance to be obtained from the German Princes without concessions on the Emperor's part, and these Frederick stubbornly declined to make. Finally, Austria claimed first attention, and till it had been recovered, Vladislas was left unassailed in Hungary.

Whatever might be the feeling in the latter country, there was no doubt as to the popularity of Maximilian's cause in Austria. Great enthusiasm prevailed, and his advance was as rapid and bloodless as it was triumphant.

Vienna University declared unanimously in his favour, and, by the end of June, 12,000 men had enlisted in his service. In July Maximilian entered Graz, and on August 19, made his triumphal entry into Vienna, which had been hastily abandoned by the Hungarian forces. The oath of allegiance was taken to Maximilian only: the citizens remembered Frederick too well to entrust themselves a second time to his mismanagement. Meanwhile Vladislas had been proclaimed King of Hungary on July 15, 1490, and in September was crowned at Stuhlweissenburg. Maximilian on this occasion displayed great activity, and, aided by a liberal grant of money from the Tyrolese Estates, invaded Hungary at the head of an army of about 17,000 men. Crossing the Raab late in October, he met with but slight opposition; Vladislas was unprepared, and by nature averse to energetic measures; and the invader was joined by a number of Hungarian magnates. But this phenomenal success was fatal to the invaders; and by the time that it reached Stuhlweissenburg, the army was virtually out of hand. In spite of a firm resistance, the city was cannonaded (Maximilian personally directing the artillery) and taken by storm; but a disgraceful scene of plunder and slaughter ensued. Maximilian and his captains were quite unable to restrain the soldiers, and on the next day an open mutiny broke out. Their refusal to advance upon Buda, and the consequent delay, proved fatal to the whole enterprise. When summoned to surrender, the capital indignantly declined, and Vladislas found time to bring up his Bohemians and to threaten Vienna. Frederick III, true to his ultra-Fabian motto—"Time ever brings its reward or its revenge"—sent no assistance, and Maximilian, seeing his base endangered, and hampered by want of money and discipline, found it necessary to withdraw westwards. His overtures to Poland met with no response, and he was quite unable to continue the struggle alone. By July 1491 Stuhlweissenburg fell into the hands of Vladislas, and all Maximilian's recent conquests were lost. The argent appeals of Reichenburg to Maximilian for reinforcements and of Maximilian to his father for money were all in vain. His position was absolutely desperate from sheer want of funds, while the turn which Breton affairs were taking seemed to render peace necessary, at whatever price. Frederick, who throughout the war had thwarted his aims and damped his ardour, now offered his mediation, and negotiations were opened in August. By the Treaty of Pressburg (November 7, 1491), Vladislas was formally recognized as King of Hungary, but, failing his lawful issue, the crown was to fall to Maximilian or his son. This promise was to be solemnly ratified by the Hungarian Estates in presence of the Imperial envoys. Moreover, Vladislas renounced all claims upon Austria, and undertook to refund Maximilian for the expenses of the war.

The old Emperor's attitude during the late war had not improved his relations with Maximilian; and the friction was rendered the more acute, when Frederick refused to see his son, and shut off various sources of income from him, thus seriously injuring his chances of success against France. Moreover, Frederick's hostility to the Bavarian Dukes formed a marked contrast to Maximilian's conciliatory position, which was mainly due to the influence of his sisterCunigunda, wife of Albert IV. Duke Albert's highhanded conduct in imposing a general tax on his subjects, in spite of the refusal of the Estates, had led to the formation of a League of discontented nobles, known as the Lowlerbund, which united with the Swabian League and was openly encouraged by the Emperor. By the end of

1491 the movement had ended in hostilities, and on January 23, 1492, Frederick III published the ban of the Empire against Duke Albert of Bavaria. The Swabian League began to arm. The French were ready to invade the Empire, if the League should attack Bavaria. An outbreak which would involve the whole of Southwest Germany seemed well-nigh inevitable, and the entire credit of the preservation of peace must rest with Maximilian. At the last moment, when the armies were actually encamped and facing each other in the field, his influence secured an adjustment of the quarrel. He had appeased his father's anger by freeing the Austrian dominions from the oath which they had taken to himself, and by referring them to the Emperor as their ruler. Frederick was now satisfied with the restoration of Regensburg to the Empire and the cancelling of Bavarian claims on Tyrol; while a full pardon was granted by Albert to all members of the Lowlerbund. (May 1492.)

Maximilian, notwithstanding this triumph of his diplomacy, met with the utmost difficulty in raising money for his operations against the French; while a new enemy had arisen in the young Charles of Egmont, who had recently recovered the Duchy of Gueldres, and who was destined to be a thorn in Maximilian's side for the rest of the reign. Though his position in West Germany was strengthened by a League with the "Lower Union", the sole result of his efforts at the Diet of Coblenz was a prospective grant of 94,000 gulden, of which only 16,000 actually came in. His campaign against the French has already been sketched. Scarcely were his hands freed by the Peace of Senlis, when an incursion of the Turks into Styria (August 1493) made a fresh demand upon his attention. Then, as usual, the necessary aid arrived too late, and the marauders returned home almost unchallenged. In the midst of this danger Frederick III, whose health had been failing for some time, and whose foot it had been found necessary to amputate, died at Linz, in the seventy-eighth year of his age (August 19, 1493).

The old Emperor had lived to see his dreams of Hapsburg revival and consolidation to a great extent realized; but his irritable nature had led him to thwart the family aspirations on Hungary. In his dread lest the acquisition of a throne should make his son more powerful than himself, he afforded him no assistance, nay rather, threw every hindrance in his way. Frederick's death was an undoubted gain to Maximilian, for it left him Emperor elect and unquestioned ruler of the Hapsburg dominions. Family divisions were no longer possible, since no relative capable of resistance survived.

But while his position was rendered more definite and imposing, there seems to have been at this period a general cooling of Maximilian's popularity, at least among the ruling classes. A powerful party in the Empire, led by Berthold of Mainz, now claimed the fulfilment of those promises of reform which he had made at the Diet of 148g, and his reluctance to devote his time to its discussion produced a distinctly bad impression among the Princes. Moreover, the part which he now began to play in Italian politics, exposing, as it did, the Imperial person to indignity and failure, roused all the old prejudices of the caste of nobles, and acted as a damper to their enthusiasm. Gladly as we should avoid threading the intricate maze of Italian politics—a task which is after all more apposite to a general history—some treatment of Maximilian's attitude during these momentous years is inevitable, even in so slight a sketch as the present. A general idea of Maximilian's ambitions in Italy will best be conveyed by his own words. "Italy has for centuries experienced what it means for the people, if no Emperor is there to restrain unruly passions, and hence the friends of the people have ever looked with favour on the Imperial power, and longed for the return of the Emperor".

The fortunes of Milan were at this moment in the hands of Ludovico il Moro, who, at first merely Regent for Gian Galeazzo, had retained the whole powers of government in his own hands, even after his nephew had come of age. The young Duke's wife, Isabella of Naples, deeply resented her husband's subordinate position, and Ludovico lived in terror of intervention on the part of Ferrante and his Florentine allies. Hoping to veil the injustice of his cause under Imperial recognition, he turned to Maximilian, and offered, in return for his own investiture as Duke of Milan, the hand of his niece, Bianca Maria Sforza, and a substantial dowry of 300,000 ducats. So much hard cash seemed to promise to the needy Maximilian the fulfilment of many a golden dream; and the bride's want of pedigree was atoned for by the practical possession of her uncle's money bags. The marriage was duly celebrated on March 9, 1494, at Halle in Tyrol, when the heir of all the Caesars linked himself with the granddaughter of a Romagnol peasant. Thus his first entry into Italian politics rightly exposed him with justice to the nickname afterwards bestowed upon him— Massimiliano Pochi Danari. "On the altar of politics the heart is often the lamb of sacrifice". Maximilian"s second marriage is not the most creditable episode in his life. The luckless Bianca Maria never filled the place of Mary in her husband's affections, and remained till her death a mere cipher, with next to no influence over him, and, though never ill-treated, entirely neglected and overlooked. The unpopularity of his marriage in Germany induced Maximilian to postpone the investiture of Ludovico with the Milanese, and GianGaleazzo dying in the interval, the Emperor was able, with less offence to his conscience, to fulfil his promise in May 1495.

Maximilian's first intention was to employ his wife's dowry in a Crusade against the Turks; and he plunged eagerly into projects of forming active alliances abroad and of raising permanent forces at home to stem the tide of infidel invasion. But disturbing rumours of the doings of Charles VIII diverted his attention to the Italian Peninsula.

By the death of Lorenzo de' Medici in 1492, the balance of power, which his skill had so long preserved in Italy, was seriously endangered. The incapable Pieroinclined towards Naples, whose attitude was now little short of openly hostile to the Milanese usurper. Ludovico, in dire need of some influential ally, made advances to the new Pope and to Venice. But his alliance with these powers was short-lived: Spanish diplomacy effected a reconciliation between Naples and Alexander VI, and Ludovico found himself more isolated than ever. The death of the old King of Naples, in January 1494, hastened events. The universal hatred with which his successor, Alfonso II, was regarded, while it drove the exiled Barons to extreme measures, was favourable to the cause of Ludovico. He turned naturally to Charles VIII, who had recently acquired the Angevin claims to the throne of Naples, and whose feeble mind was filled with all the clap-trap of mediaeval chivalry. The appeal met with an enthusiastic response: every other trend of policy was sacrificed that this might succeed. By the end of August 1494, all was prepared for the invasion of Italy, and, with a magnificently appointed army of 60,000 men, Charles crossed the Alps and was welcomed by the traitor Ludovico. Florence opened her gates to the deliverer : the Pope abandoned Rome at his approach, and looked on in sullen anxiety from Sant' Angelo; and Naples itself was occupied amid general rejoicings, almost before a single blow had been struck.

Dazzled by such unprecedented success, Charles VIII lost all restraint and began to indulge in the wildest dreams. He was to recover Jerusalem, to eject the infidel from Europe, and to restore in his own person the fallen Empire of Constantinople. Rightly or wrongly, he was credited with the intention of forcing the Pope to crown him Emperor of the West, or of driving him from the Papal throne and instituting a thorough reform of the Church. Such rumours could not but fill Maximilian with an uneasiness which Borgia's letters did not fail to augment. It was only owing to the skilful diplomacy of Charles' envoys and his own strained relations with Venice, that he preserved neutrality for so long as he did. Had not others taken alarm at the turn of affairs, he might have prevaricated till the time for action had passed. Ludovico, who was before all others responsible for the French expedition, was the first to be disillusioned. Alarmed at the open designs of the Duke of Orleans on Milan, he soon became as anxious for Charles' ruin as he had been eager for his success, and looked for assistance to his more powerful neighbours. But it was Ferdinand of Spain who really brought about Maximilian's change of policy, by holding out the tempting bait of a double marriage alliance with his House. The Emperor's suspicions of Venice were overcome, and the Signoria became the centre of opposition to France. The various intrigues were conducted with such skill and secrecy, that even Comines, who then held the post of French Ambassador in Venice, was completely outwitted. But their details do not leave us with a favourable impression of the confederates' straightforwardness. The itch of the Republic's patriotic palm was allayed by a promise of the Apulian ports; while the Pope displayed to the full his talent for shifty intrigue and prevarication, and Maximilian kept up a stream of friendly assurances which effectively duped his young and incapable rival.

Thus the proclamation of the Holy League, between the Pope, Maximilian, Ferdinand, Ludovico and the Venetians, (March 31, 1495) came upon the French as a bolt from the blue. Its ostensible objects were to defend the Papacy, and to secure peace in Italy and mutual protection against the attacks of other Princes. But from the very first its members made little attempt to conceal their genuine aim—the expulsion of the French from the Peninsula. The massing of troops by each of the allies removed all doubts upon the subject; and Charles VIII saw himself compelled to abandon Naples. On July 6, 1495, he encountered the forces of the League at the battle of Fornovo, and after a running engagement made good his retreat westwards. Even then the German and Venetian troops might have inflicted serious losses on his armies ere they recrossed the Alps; but the treachery of Ludovico, who concluded a treaty with Charles without consulting any of his allies, forced them to retire and leave the French unmolested.

Meanwhile Maximilian was engaged at the famous Diet of Worms (26 March-August, 1495). Burning to strike a blow which might tend to the humiliation of his rival, he found himself once more, so to speak, the prisoner of his pocket. The Electors and the other Estates were determined that redress should precede supply, and stubbornly refused to grant a single florin, until the question of reform had been placed on a satisfactory basis. Nor can they be accused of any want of patriotism; for the interests of the Empire were by no means coincident with those of Austria. Indeed, had not Maximilian's territorial instincts triumphed so completely over his feelings as Emperor, he might have been the first to recognize the deep and sterling patriotism which inspired the Elector Berthold. As it was, his first intention had been to remain fourteen days at Worms, and, after obtaining the Diet's sanction for the Imperial levies, to conduct a vigorous campaign against the French. But here he was met by the practical impossibility of inducing a body mainly constituted for peace, to undertake a long and tedious war at a distance. The feudal system had fallen into decay, and the old military power of the Empire was no more. New circumstances demanded new measures; and the triumph achieved by a standing army in France pointed the direction which military reform should take. The proposal, then, which Maximilian laid before the Diet, was for a continuous money aid for ten or twelve years; with this he might form an army of landsknechts. But the Diet was wholly unsympathetic, and rigidly confined itself to schemes of reform. Meetings were sometimes held without any reference to the Emperor, and, as he indignantly exclaimed, he found himself treated with less consideration than some petty burgomaster. The struggle of parties lasted throughout the summer, Maximilian adopting a highly undignified attitude of sulking. On three occasions he was particularly pressing, especially in August, when Novara was threatened by the Swiss, and a mutiny of the landsknechts might be expected, if their pay was not forthcoming. At last nothing was left for Maximilian but submission, and he accepted the Elector Berthold's proposals for reform. But Charles VIII had already recrossed the Alps, and the time for action was past.

Yet, notwithstanding his enforced inactivity, Maximilian's presence at Worms had not been in vain. The brilliancy of the Court and the gallant ceremonies of the lists hid from the casual observer the true meaning of this great assembly of princes and nobles. Yet the two important results of Maximilian's policy form a striking contrast to his humiliation at the hands of the Electors. In return for the services of Count Eberhard he erected Wurtemberg into a Duchy, at the same time limiting the succession to heirs-male. Since the hopes of the new ducal family rested upon one delicate youth, this arrangement held out to Maximilian or his successors the prospect of acquiring the fair valley of the upper Neckar. But the other achievement of his policy was destined to have far more momentous consequences. This was the fulfilment of his agreement with Ferdinand the Catholic, in accordance with which the Prince of Asturias was betrothed to Margaret of Austria, and the Archduke Philip to Joanna of Spain. By an extraordinary fatality, the latter marriage, which at the time had seemed the less important of the two, came to exercise a vast influence on the history of Europe. The Spanish heir died within a year of his marriage (1497), and Margaret's child lived but a few days. Isabella Queen of Portugal was now heiress of Castile and Arragon; but the fates fought against the unity of the Peninsula. In 1498 Isabella died, and in 1500 her only child, Prince Miguel, followed her to the grave. Philip's wife, Joanna, became heiress of Spain and all its splendid dependencies in the New World.

Though Maximilian had been thwarted in the hope of meeting his rival on the open field, the next year brought a prospect of intervention in Italian affairs. Charles VIII, on his return to France, had set on foot preparations for a fresh invasion. The success of his overtures to the Swiss Cantons, and the servile attitude of Florence, filled the Venetians and Ludovico with alarm; and the two powers invited Maximilian to make an expedition to Italy in person. His eagerness to restore Imperial influence in that country, coupled with his knightly thirst for renown, led him, with curious inconsistency, to submit to the indignity of becoming the pensioner of States whose feudal superior he claimed to be. Each promised 30,000 ducats for three months towards the payment of his troops and engaged a number of Swiss mercenaries in addition. The Emperor's sanguine nature already saw the French party in Italy crushed, and frontier provinces wrested from the grasp of Charles. But the Estates of the Empire, which had been summoned to meet at Lindau, proved more unmanageable than ever. Even had his condottiere-contract not filled them with disgust, they were wholly disinclined to repay his grudging and half-cancelled concessions by grants of money for an object which the Empire viewed with indifference. His penury may be judged by a letter which he received from his councillors at Worms, containing an urgent request for more money, as the maintenance of the courtiers has been stopped, and the Queen and her ladies will be provided for "only three or four days more; and if within that time no money comes, even their food-supplies will come to an end".

Charles VIII's financial straits soon compelled him to abandon his schemes of active interference in Italy; and the Signoria, no longer needing Maximilian's presence, now came to regard him as a positive hindrance to their aggrandizing policy. But nothing could divert him from his project. When the Venetians boggled over their promised subsidy, he secured the necessary sum by loans from theFuggers. The remonstrances of his advisers were of none avail. At Augsburg and Linz he divided his time between wild dreams of conquest with the Archduke Philip, and the festive entertainments of the citizens. On St. John's Eve he led the fairest maiden of the town to the dance, and gallantly assisted her to kindle the bonfire, to the sound of drums and cornets and the merry music of the dance. In July he had an interview with Ludovico at Münster, receiving him in hunting dress, surrounded by his companions of the chase; and in the last days of August entered Italy by the Valtelline. Even then his compact was not strictly fulfilled. Instead of the stipulated 7,000 men, his army never amounted to more than 4,000. His first scheme, of driving the French from Asti and forcing Savoy to join the League, was sacrificed to the jealousy of Venice, which opposed any increase of the power of Milan. Nor were his own relations with Ludovico distinguished by their cordiality. The latter declined to subsidize him unless the Pope and Venice granted equal amounts, and sought to employ him in garrisoning the Milanese against French attacks. Finally, Maximilian decided upon an attack on Florence, and as a preliminary laid siege to Livorno, curtly informing Ludovico that if he would not provide money for his troops he had better dismiss them to their homes. But the numbers of the besiegers were insufficient for the task, the Venetians held aloof, and the French garrison never lost entire command of the sea. The arrival of a fleet from Marseilles removed Maximilian's last hopes of reducing the city; his resources were by now exhausted, and, declaring that "against the will of God and men he would not wage this war", he hurriedly retired northwards. He turned a deaf ear to the entreaties of the Papal Legate, and before Christmas was again in Tyrol. According to the Italian wits, not even hunting invitations could detain the disappointed monarch. In short his conduct presents a favourable opportunity for introducing the cricitisms of Quirini, one of the first of that line of brilliant ambassadors, whose diplomacy prolonged the existence of Venice till modern times. "He is of excellent parts, and more fertile in expedients than any of his advisers, yet he does not know how to avail himself of any single remedy at the right moment; while he is as full of ideas and plans as he is powerless to execute them. And though two or three methods lie open to his intellect, and though he chooses one of them as the best, yet he does not pursue this, because before itsfulfilment another design which he considers better has suddenly presented itself. And thus he went from better to better, till both time and opportunity for execution are past!". Yet with all his indecision and want of perseverance, he was resigned and cheerful in adversity, and it was perhaps at this period that he consoled himself with the assurance "Gott sorgt schon: es könnte noch schlimmergehen".

Maximilian's failure left the French influence all-powerful in Italy; but Charles VIII made no further movement, and his premature death in April 1498 materially changed the situation. The first act of Louis XI—his infamous divorce from Jeanne of France, followed by his marriage to Anne of Brittany—can hardly have been gratifying news to Maximilian. Still, the latter hoped to obtain the restoration of Burgundy from the new King, in return for acquiescence in the French policy in Italy. But when his representations met with no response, he sought aid from the Diet for a war against France. In spite of its refusal, and though he might have seen that the League had no intention of pulling his chestnuts out of the fire, he threw an army into Burgundy. But the Swiss mercenaries, who formed its strength, either were bribed by Louis or mutinied for want of pay; while Philip concluded a separate peace with France (July 2, 1499), actually renouncing the claims which his father brought forward in his name, and receiving from Louis XII the investiture of Artois and Flanders. The French King was led to conclude this treaty by his designs upon the Duchy of Milan, which he claimed as the lawful heir of the Visconti dynasty. His wise policy of treating the various members of the League as though it were non-existent was crowned with success. Ere long all were pacified but Maximilian, and he was rendered harmless by systematic intriguing with the Swiss Confederates—a policy which had a perceptible influence in producing the memorable Swiss war of 1499. The immediate causes of the outbreak were incidents of petty friction on the Tyrolese border; but the real question at issue was the relation of the Confederates to the Empire.

No sooner had the Swiss in earlier days attained their object of holding directly from the Emperor, than they made it sufficiently obvious that this dependence was for the future to be mainly nominal. During the long reign of Frederick III they had enjoyed just such a state of internal peace and order as the perpetual Landfriede and the Kammergericht aimed at securing for the rest of the Empire; and now, when Maximilian demanded their submission to the decrees of the Diet of Worms, by contributing men and money for his schemes of foreign policy, war was practically inevitable. Their close relations with successive Kings of France had long shown the slight regard in which they held their nominal ruler. Their connection with the Empire brought them no advantage, submision to the Common Penny (das Gemeine Pfennig) naturally appeared a hardship to them, and the decisions of the Kammergericht they regarded as assaults upon their treasured freedom. Their refusal of Maximilian's demands was coupled with general steps for union with the sister Leagues of the Graubünden and the Valais. The war began with marauding and skirmishing, growing fiercer and assuming larger proportions when the Swabian League armed itself at the Imperial summons. But the Swiss everywhere held their own : their superiority was admitted even by the Count ofFürstenberg, general of the League, who branded his own troops as "ein flüchtig,schnöd und ehrlos Volk". Maximilian himself had been engaged in unprofitable operations against the Duke of Gueldres, and only arrived upon the scene in July, to find matters going against him. Even his presence did not turn the balance, and at Schwaderloch the Swiss, though somewhat outnumbered, more than held their own. Only four days later (July 24), the army of Henry of Fürstenberg, 15,000 to 16,000 strong, suffered a severe defeat at Dornach at the hands of 6,000 Confederates. The Austrian leader, with many distinguished nobles and about 4,000 men, perished on the field. This disaster dealt the final blow to Maximilian's hopes. At first he shut himself up in the Castle of Lindau, and refused to see any of his nobles. But he soon reconciled himself to the necessity of coming to terms.

The Treaty of Basel (September 22, 1499), though less

remarkable for its provisions than for its omissions, is one of the landmarks of Swiss history. By it mutual conquests were restored, and Maximilian recovered the Prattigau, while various small disputes were referred to arbitration. But, while Swiss independence was not formally recognized by the Empire till a century and a half later, it was tacitly secured by this treaty; and henceforward the Confederates enjoyed entire immunity from Imperial jurisdiction and from Imperial taxation. Nor was this the only result of the struggle. The Swiss had won for themselves a position which inspired their neighbours with a genuine admiration and a very wholesome fear. Respected and courted by the outer world, they strengthened their position internally by a close union of the Confederates and the Graubünden. The Empire was deprived for ever of a number of its most valuable subjects, and the House of Hapsburg was finally excluded from the cradle of its greatness. No one reaped fuller advantage from the Swiss war than Louis XII. While all the energies of Maximilian were devoted to coping with the Confederates, he found himself free to carry into execution his projected invasion of the Milanese. Had the Emperor proved successful, Ludovico might perhaps have saved himself (or at least prolonged the struggle) by entering the Swabian League; but with the defeat ofDornach the usurper's fate was sealed. Louis XII, who had already allied himself with the Pope and Venice, winning the support of the latter by the promise of Cremona, crossed the Alps at the end of July with an army of 22,000 men, and entered Milan almost unopposed. Ludovico, deserted and betrayed by his people, sought refuge in Tyrol, and was among the first to bring the tidings of his own misfortunes to his Imperial nephew. But though received with the utmost sympathy and respect by Maximilian, he soon perceived that the latter was as usual at the end of his resources, and that no assistance need be looked for from him. He purchased the services of 8,000 Swiss mercenaries and of the celebratedBurgundian guard, and with their aid recovered his capital and most of its territory. But the army which Louis XII despatched to the assistance of Bayard consisted largely of Swiss troops; and Ludovico's mercenaries, refusing to fight against their countrymen in the French service, renounced his cause and betrayed him to the enemy (April 10, 1500). In this undignified way one of the chief disturbers of the peace of Italy bids a last farewell to the field of politics; he remained in the most rigorous confinement at Loches for the next five years, after which the earnest intercession of Maximilian secured some relaxation in his treatment. He was allowed a space of several leagues around his prison for hunting and other amusements, and died in captivity in 1510.

On the very day when Ludovico fell into the hands of the French, Maximilian opened the Imperial Diet at Augsburg. His main object was to obtain aid against France; but the complete failure of his recent military enterprises—alike in Burgundy, Gueldres, Switzerland and Milan—compelled him to acquiesce in the formation of a Council of Regency, (Reichsregiment), which was to discuss all military and financial affairs, and even questions of foreign policy, which at that period were considered the special department of the Monarch. This Council consisted of twenty-one members, of whom sixteen were appointed by the Electors and Princes, two by the Imperial towns; while Maximilian nominated two for Austria and Burgundy, and only one, the President, in his capacity of Emperor. The promoters of the scheme aimed at little short of his abdication; while he, on his part, cheerfully assumed that they would defer to his wishes on matters of foreign politics. The bait held out to him by Berthold was a permanent war administration, possessing power both to levy troops and to impose taxes; from this he promised himself an army of 30,000 men, and money to maintain it. But the project remained upon paper, and Maximilian's disgust was turned to fury when the first step of the new Council was to conclude a truce with France, and virtually to commit him to investing Louis XII with Milan. Finding himself helpless in view of the Diet's opposition, and determined not to submit to the ruling of the Council, he began to make separate overtures to the French King. In this he was readily encouraged by the Archduke Philip and by Ferdinand, who was already hatching his iniquitous plot for the partition of Naples, and who found Maximilian's hostile attitude to France a drag upon Louis' action. In October 1501 the visit of Cardinal d'Amboise, the trusted adviser of Louis XII, to the Court of Innsbruck, brought matters to a final issue. A treaty, whose friendliness was only rivalled by its hypocrisy, was concluded between the two Monarchs. The infant Archduke Charles was betrothed to Louis' daughter Claude; Louis himself was to receive the investiture of Milan, in return for the sum of 80,000 crowns, and promised to assist the Emperor in his journey to Rome and in his projects against the Turks. But the actual terms of the agreement were of little importance, as they were obviously intended only for momentary ends. The conquest of Naples, which was effected in the years E501 1505, soon led to quarrels between the two conquerors. Louis XII's continual intrigues with the German Princes induced Maximilian to support the Spanish cause by the despatch of 2,500 landsknechts; and by the end of 1504 the brilliant tactics of the great Captain resulted in the final expulsion of the French from the kingdom of Naples. At the same time the Emperor found means to check Louis' intrigues, which the outbreak of the Bavarian war had rendered dangerous. By the Treaty of Blois (September 22), Milan was ensured to Louis XII, and, failing heirs-male, to Claude and her youthful bridegroom Charles. But this agreement, like its predecessor, was not made to be observed. No sooner had d'Amboise obtained Louis' formal investiture from the Emperor (April 1505), than the betrothal of Claude to the Archduke was secretly annulled, and Francis of Angouleme took his place as her prospective husband. The death of Isabella the Catholic, and the struggle of Ferdinand and Philip for the Castilian Regency, removed all danger of any united effort between Spain and the Hapsburgs against France; and early in 1506 Louis' breach of faith was formally proclaimed and ratified by the States-General of Tours.

Notwithstanding this rebuff, Maximilian had gained a very distinct advantage from peace with France. So long as the question of investiture was pending, Louis could not interfere in the affairs of the Empire, and Maximilian was free to profit by the turn of events.

The death of George the Rich, Duke of Bavaria-Landshut (December 1, 1503), resulted in a disputed succession. In spite of a family agreement (Erbvertrag) which expressly nominated as his heirs Duke Albert IV of Munich and his brother Wolfgang, the old Duke left his lands to his daughter Elizabeth, wife of Rupert, a younger son of the Elector Palatine. Both parties prepared to assert their rights, and Rupert, careless of the consequences, threw himself into Landshut, thus opening the war, and putting himself under the ban of the Empire. The Estates refused allegiance to Albert, and called in Maximilian as mediator in the quarrel. The Emperor preferred to renounce his position of *tertius gaudens,* and to throw the whole weight of his support on Albert's side. Even had he not already, in 1497, recognized Albert's title, both justice and his own interests urged him to the Bavarian side. The Palatine House had ever been the foe of the Hapsburgs, and Duke Albert, as the Emperor's brother-in-law, would naturally seem the less dangerous of the two claimants. Maximilian at first offered Rupert a third of George's possessions, in the hope of averting hostilities; but, meeting with a curt refusal, he roused the forces of the Swabian League, and, assisted by Würtemberg, Brunswick and Hesse, took the field in person at the head of a considerable army. The sudden death of Rupert (August 20, 1504), closely followed by that of his masculine wife Elizabeth, did not put an end to the war, the Elector continuing the struggle in the name of his grandsons. A fierce encounter took place near Regensburg between the Imperialists and a large body of Bohemian mercenaries in the Elector's service. Maximilian himself led the right wing to the charge, and drove the enemy back to their laager, which, after the example of Zizka, they had constructed from their baggage waggons. A desperate sally for the moment broke the Imperialist ranks, and he was surrounded and dragged from his horse by the long grappling hooks attached to the Bohemians' lances. He owed his life to the distinguished gallantry of Eric of Brunswick, who scattered his assailants when all hope seemed lost. Rallying his troops, he led them on to victory, and defeated the enemy with heavy loss. This affray was followed up by the siege of Kufstein, in which the Emperor's artillery played an important part—especially two heavy pieces, which he had christened "Purlepaus" and "Weckauf von Oesterreich". The hesitation of the garrison, which at first made promises of surrender, and then decided upon resistance, so deeply incensed Maximilian, that when the inevitable capitulation came, he refused to show any mercy. It was only when half the scanty garrison had been executed that the intercession of the Princes prevailed to secure pardon for such as remained (October 17, 1504). The capture of Kufstein was the last serious incident of the war. A truce was concluded in February, 1505, and in August, when Maximilian appeared at the Diet of Köln, he was able to dictate his own terms to the discomfited Elector. With the exception of Neuburg, and some territory north of the Danube, which were formed into an appanage for Rupert's children, all the lands of George were made over to Bavaria. But the Emperor had not conducted the war solely from the kindness of his heart, and both claimed and secured a substantial reward for his services. From the Palatinate he acquiredHagenau and the Ortenau; from Bavaria, Kufstein, Rattenberg, and a number of petty lordships, and, most important of all, the Zillerthal, which gave Tyrol a strong frontier to the northeast, and rounded off the territories to which he had succeeded in 1500 on the death of Leonard of Görz.

Maximilian's reputation in the Empire was now perhaps higher than it had ever been before; the more so, that in the winter of 1504 death had removed his old opponent, Berthold of Mainz, and that the new Elector was a near relative of his own. But when the future was all bright with hope, and when his coronation at Rome and an union of Spain and the Empire against the French and the Turks seemed at last on the point of realization, his golden dreams met with a rude awakening. The sudden and premature death of Philip, who had assumed in person the government of Castile, and was successfully defending himself against the spiteful intrigues of Ferdinand, put an end to the Emperor's projects of Hapsburg combination (Sep. 25, 1506). The Catholic King recovered the Regency, and was soon more powerful than ever in the Spanish Peninsula. Maximilian at first met with no better success in his attempt to secure the government of the Low Countries. The Estates of the seventeen Provinces refused to recognize his claims to the Regency during the minority of his grandson Charles, and were encouraged by Louis XII in the formation of a Council of Regency. But internal troubles, and the activity of Charles of Gueldres, pled his cause more eloquently than any measures of his own. On their voluntary submission to his rule, he appointed William de Croy, Lord of Chievres, and Adrian of Utrecht as Charles' tutors, and entrusted the administration to his daughter Margaret, the widowed Duchess of Savoy, who made her public entry into Mechlin in July 1507, and who throughout her rule justified his choice by her scrupulous integrity and brilliant statesmanship.

In the same year, 1507, Maximilian made a fiery appeal to the Diet assembled at Constance, for assistance in his schemes of a journey to Rome and the expulsion of the French from Milan. After considerable delay he obtained a grant of 3,000 horse 9,000 foot for six months, and received a further promise of 6,000 men from the Swiss envoys. But his sanguine expectations were once more doomed to disappointment. The majority of the promised troops never made their appearance; French gold won over his Swiss allies; and the Estates of his own dominions outdid all previous occasions in their parsimony. Meanwhile his ardent preparations had roused the distrust of Venice, which refused him passage through her dominions, unless he restricted himself to a trifling escort.

His army was too weak to force its way either through Milanese or through Venetian territory; and hence he was driven to an expedient which involved a break with the old mediaeval traditions of the Empire. On February 4, 1508, he had himself proclaimed with great pomp and solemnity, in the Cathedral of Trent, as Holy Roman Emperor. It was declared that for the future in all official documents he should be known by the title of "erwählte römischer Kaiser", but that for convenience sake he should commonly be called "Emperor". Julius II raised no objection, partly because Maximilian fully acknowledged the Papal right to crown him, and still more because his arrival in Rome with an army would have been a most unwelcome event. Maximilian's step was the first departure from the immemorial custom of his predecessors; but with the exception of his grandson, Charles V, not one of his successors in the Empire received his crown at the hands of the Pope.

The refusal of Venice to grant a passage to the Imperial army accentuated the ill-feeling which had long existed between Maximilian and the Republic. Now that his ambitions could find no outlet to the South, he turned his gaze Eastwards, and rashly embroiled himself with his powerful neighbour. Within a month of his assumption of the Imperial dignity, his troops were advancing into Venetian territory from three different directions, threatening Vicenza, the valley of the Adige, and Friuli. Maximilian gives expression to his rosy dreams of victory in a letter to the Elector of Saxony : "The Venetians paint their lion with two feet in the sea, the third on the plains, the fourth on the mountains. We have almost won the foot on the mountains, only one claw is wanting, which with God's help we shall have in eight days; then we mean to conquer the foot on the plains too". But the very day after this confident epistle was penned, Trautson, one of his best captains, was routed and killed by the Venetians, with a total loss of over 2,000. The Venetians now took the offensive in earnest, and, superior both in numbers and discipline, completely turned the tables on the Imperialists. Town after town fell before their advance, and by the end of June, Görz, Pordenone, Adelsberg, Trieste were in their hands; while the fleet seized Fiume and overawed the whole of Istria. As soon as the tide began to turn, Maximilian had hastened back to Germany, to rouse the Electors and the Swabian League, but from neither could he obtain any real assistance. The whole brunt of the defence fell upon the Tyrolese, who responded manfully to the call, and checked the Venetian advance at Pietra, on the way to Trent. But any prolonged resistance was hopeless; and Maximilian saw himself obliged to conclude a three years' truce with the Republic, by which the latter retained all her conquests except Adelsberg.

The Emperor's humiliation at the hands of Venice only served to augment the suspicion and dislike with which she was regarded by her other neighbours. The Pope felt an especial grudge against her, as the possessor of Ravenna and Rimini, which lawfully belonged to the Holy See. Already in the summer of 1507 he had been feeling his way towards a coalition, by an attempt to restore friendly relations between Louis and Maximilian; but the latter was then still too full of schemes for the recovery of Milan to entertain the proposal. When however he engaged in war with Venice, he sent agents of his own accord to Louis XII. The latter at first refused all accommodation unless Venice were included; but when the Republic neglected to include Gueldres in the truce, he availed himself of this flimsy excuse to negotiate with the Emperor. An active exchange of views followed between Margaret and her father, both as to an agreement with France, with regard to which he trusted largely to her judgment, and the proposed marriage of Charles with Mary of England, to which he would only consent in return for a substantial loan. Maximilian himself arrived in the Netherlands in August, but does not seem to have visited his daughter. When the crisis of the negotiations was reached he still remained in the background, and deputed Margaret and his councillor, Matthew Lang, to receive the French envoys at Cambrai. D'Amboise raised so many difficulties that at length Margaret threatened to return home, declaring that they were merely wasting time. This firm attitude brought the French envoys to reason, and on December 10, 1508, the memorable League of Cambrai was duly ratified. Ostensibly it was a renewal of the treaties of 1501 and 1504, with the exception of the betrothal of Claude and Charles. But its genuine aim was the complete partition of the Venetian land-Empire between the four arch-conspirators. The Pope was to receive the towns of the Romagna, Ferdinand the Apulian seaports. Maximilian was to recover all his lost territories and to supplement them by Verona, Padua, Vicenza, Treviso and Friuli; while Louis XII should occupy Brescia, Bergamo and Cremona. The Imperial conscience, which felt some scruples at so prompt an infringement of the truce, was saved by the commands of Julius II, who bade him, as protector of the Church, take part in the recovery of her lands. Further, to veil the iniquity of the agreement, the Pope excommunicated Venice and all its subject lands.

Though Maximilian thus isolated Venice, and made it possible to recover his lost territory, yet his adhesion to the

League was an undoubted political error. Not only did his action assist the destruction of the only power in North Italy capable of resisting the foreigner, and thus directly lead to the establishment of French predominance in Lombardy; but it also implanted in the minds of the Signoria that irremovable distrust of his intentions which was responsible for many of his later misfortunes, and which the pursuance of a straightforward policy might have averted. Had he exercised but a moderate amount of foresight, he would have realized that Louis, with his vast superiority in power and resources, would sooner or later discard his needy ally and reserve the lion's share for himself. It is probable that the false glamour and vanity of the Imperial tradition obscured his eyes to the fact of his own weakness; and what from one point of view is his strength—his unquenchable hopefulness and buoyancy of spirit—here proved his weakness and egged him on to defeat and humiliation.

Leaving the Netherlands after a year's residence, Maximilian repaired to the Diet of Worms (April, 1509). Never before had the Estates been so unanimous in refusing all support and loading him with complaints. The cities were enraged at the practical supersession of the Council of Regency, the Princes at his negotiating without their consent. After mutual recriminations, they separated without effecting anything; and their dispersal marks the end of all genuine attempts at Reform. Even Maximilian's hereditary Estates voted far fewer men than he had expected, and qualified even this grant by making the troops liable to service only when he was personally in command. He thus found himself involved in a serious war, without having sufficient resources to execute his far-reaching designs, and was reduced to pledge tolls, mines, and other sources of revenue in order to raise money.

The first great incident of the war was the Battle of Agnadello (May 14, 1509), in which the Venetians suffered defeat at the hands of the French. The Papal troops occupied Ravenna and the rest of the Romagna, while Ferdinand added theApulian ports to his new dominions. For the first and last time Venice made Maximilian a really advantageous offer: all his lands should be restored, the Imperial suzerainty should be recognized, and a handsome yearly subsidy paid down. But the envoys of the Republic were not even allowed to approach him, and about midsummer the Emperor opened the campaign in person with 15,000 men. The Venetians had drawn off the mass of their troops to meet the French advance, and he was virtually unopposed. By the middle of July he had recovered all that he had lost, and occupied in addition Verona, Vicenza, Padua, Bassano and Feltre. He had already fetched some heavy artillery over the Brenner to reduce Treviso, when the complexion of affairs was suddenly and completely reversed. The inhabitants of the invaded districts remained loyal to the Venetians, and so many of the Imperial troops were required to check their harassing movements that the towns were insufficiently garrisoned. The Pope and Ferdinand, their own objects once attained, grew indifferent to the progress of the League, and the Venetians bravely rallied and by a sudden movement regained possession of Padua. The Emperor, leaving Treviso, laid siege to Padua with some 22,000 men, and employed his heavy ordnance with considerable effect. But the numbers of the garrison prevented him from maintaining a complete blockade; and when two brilliant and determined assaults had failed to reduce the town, he raised the siege and returned to Tyrol (October). He himself explains his action by the great number of troops and artillery inside, by the wonderful strength of the defences, and by the lukewarm spirit of his own troops. But the main reasons are to be found in the short period for which the troops were voted, and the entire lack of money to win them for further services. Even in August the Emperor was pawning "deux couliers d'orgarniz de beaucop de bonnes et riches pierres", and a number of other valuable jewels. The Venetians quickly recovered all places of any importance, with the solitary exception of Verona, which was defended by a mixed garrison of Germans, French and Spaniards. Maximilian, at the end of his resources, threw himself unreservedly into the hands of Louis XII.

The Diet of Augsburg, which met in January, 1510, would have acted wisely in strengthening his hands; for, now that there was a danger of both Italy and the Papacy becoming dependent upon France, it was more than ever to the interests of Germany to hold a strong position south of the Alps. In spite of his rash onsets without adequate preparation, Maximilian had a strong sense of the greatness of the Empire, and was pre-eminently fitted to rouse the patriotism of Germany in a struggle against the foreigner. The Diet did, it is true, vote 1,800 horse and 6,000 foot for six months, but it had taken four months to make up its mind to the sacrifice, and even then the troops never arrived. Meanwhile the League had broken up. Julius II, once in possession of the Romagnan cities, devoted himself to the problem of "the expulsion of the barbarian". With this end in view, he removed the ban from the Republic (February, 1510) and concluded a five years' league with the Swiss, who were to send 6,000 mercenaries to his aid. In July the Papal and Venetian armies assumed the offensive, and the latter were able to reoccupy Friuli. But Julius met with disaster on all sides; Maximilian and Louis won over the Swiss to inactivity, and Henry VIII, on whose aid the Pope had reckoned, made peace with France. Maximilian's attitude towards Venice was fiercer and more hostile than ever, and led him to encourage the Pasha of Bosnia to attack her Adriatic possessions. He himself declares that he hopes soon "to carry out some fine exploit and execution against our enemy; for it is not enough to put them to death by the hundred: we must dispose of them by the thousand". Julius was driven to modify or conceal his contemptuous opinion of the Emperor, whom he had treated to the nick-name of "a naked baby". For it was mainly through the latter's influence that the Congress of Mantua was arranged, and attended by the envoys of France, Spain, England and the Pope (March 1511), the primary object being the restoration of the League against Venice. Earnest negotiations were also conducted at Bologna between the Pope and Matthew Lang, who loyally resisted the bribes of a cardinal's hat from Julius and of large subsidies from Venice. The disproportion between the demands of the Emperor and the Republic was too great to be overcome, and the Pope's hopes of winning Maximilian to his League were frustrated. Still powerless by himself, Maximilian was more than ever dependent on the French, and played a somewhat subordinate part in the operations of Louis against the Venetians. Adespatch which he received from Trivulzio shows us in what scanty consideration he was held by the French commander. Referring to the capture of Mirandola by a German captain, he declares that "it has thrown me into a worse humour than I have been in during my life", and denounces the Imperialists in the most outspoken fashion.

The sudden illness of Julius II (August 1511), from which a fatal issue was generally expected, led to an episode, which, though trivial in itself and void of result, gives us a vivid impression of Maximilian's visionary nature. He actually entertained the preposterous idea of himself succeeding Julius and uniting Empire and Papacy in one person. Lang, Bishop of Gurk, was to proceed at once to Rome, to persuade the Pope "to take us as coadjutor, so that on his death we may be assured of having the Papacy, and of becoming a priest, and afterwards a saint, so that after my death you will be constrained to adore me, whence I shall gain much glory". If necessary, Lang was to spend 300,000 ducats in bribing the various Cardinals, and Maximilian counted upon the assistance of Ferdinand and the people of Rome. His confidential letter to Margaret bears the signature— "vostrebon père Maximilian, futur pape". But these extravagant dreams were dissipated by the unexpected recovery of Julius II, who plunged more eagerly than ever into political life. On October 5, 1511, the Holy League was openly published in Rome. Its members—the Pope, Ferdinand and Venice—veiled their real design, the expulsion of the French, under the sanctimonious pretence of maintaining the integrity of the Papal States. Throughout the early stages of the war Maximilian remained virtually inactive, but steadily declined to desert his French allies. But none the less he permitted Ferdinand and the Pope to conclude in his name a ten months' truce with Venice. He was thus in the happy position of being in request with both sides, while himself free from all immediate danger. When the death of Gaston de Foix at Ravenna (April 11, 1512) deprived the French of their most capable leader, and the tide began to turn against them, Maximilian inclined towards the side of the Pope. In allowing 18,000 Swiss to pass through Tyrol on their way to join the Venetians, and in issuing strict orders that all Germans serving with Louis should return home, he was certainly guilty of unfriendly conduct towards his ally. In the actual expulsion of the French from the Milanese he took no direct part, but from want of funds rather than disinclination,—the Diet of Trier turning a deaf ear to his most urgent entreaties. At length in November he took the decisive step. Though he had hoped to see Milan under his grandson Charles rather than Massimiliano Sforza, he consented to a league with Julius II, to whom the Imperial recognition of the Lateran Council was of vital importance. In return for this the Pope promised his support against Venice, with temporal as well as spiritual arms.

In February 1513, however, the situation was again changed by the death of Julius II, and by the reconciliation of France and Venice. The new Pope, Leo X, was vacillating and untrustworthy, though nominally well-disposed to the Emperor; and the latter began to turn elsewhere for an ally. On April 5, 1513, a treaty of alliance was concluded between Maximilian and Henry VIII, mainly through the efforts of Margaret, who had long urged on her father a break with France and a close union with Spain and England. At first we find him complaining that Henry "gives us only to understand what he wishes from us, while of what he ought to do for us there is no mention". But the promise of 100,0oo gold crowns was magical in its effect; all his opposition ceased, and he indulged in the usual sanguine anticipations. Ferdinand, Henry and Maximilian would unite until France was completely crushed, and by a joint invasion would win back all the territories which had been wrested from their ancestors. The alliance was to be cemented at the earliest possible date by the marriage of

Charles to Mary of England.

Notwithstanding such threatening signs, the French king pushed on his preparations for a new invasion of Italy. The rapid success of the expedition was suddenly effaced on the field of Novara (June 6, 1513), where the French sustained a severe defeat at the hands of the Swiss and were driven back across the Alps. Their return to France virtually coincided with the expedition of Henry VIII. At the end of June the English army landed at Calais, and marching in three divisions, appeared before Térouenne on August 1. Eleven days later he was joined by Maximilian, who had already announced his intention of serving as the English king's chief captain. "His experienced eye at once detected a capital blunder in Henry's strategic position", but the lethargy and exhaustion of the French had saved the latter from any awkward consequences. The French armies had suffered terribly at Novara, and Louis XII himself was too broken in health to infuse vigourinto the operations. On August 16, Maximilian, at the head of the allied forces, won a brilliant little victory at Guinegate, the scene of his earlier triumph over the French in 1479. The enemy's headlong retreat won for the engagement the familiar name of the Battle of Spurs. This resulted in the surrender of Térouenne, whose example was followed on September 24 by the important town of Tournai. But, in spite of Maximilian's eager encouragement, Henry VIII refused to make full use of his advantage. The lateness of the season, the difficulties of obtaining sufficient supplies, and still more the position of affairs in Scotland, made him anxious to return to England; and in November he re-embarked his army, leaving vague promises of a renewal of the campaign in the following spring. Maximilian's disappointment had been seriously augmented by the course of events on theBurgundian frontier. Towards the end of August an army of 30,000 Swiss and Germans, led by Ulric of Würtemberg, had penetrated into Burgundy, and on September 7 laid siege to Dijon. A determined assault upon the town came within an ace of success, and made it clear to La Trémouille, the commander of the garrison, that any prolonged resistance was impossible. Substantial bribes to the Swiss leaders won over the invaders to a treaty, by which Louis XII was to make peace with the Pope, to evacuate Milan, Cremona and Asti in favour of the young Sforza, and to pay 400,000 crowns to the Swiss. On the strength of this agreement Burgundy was evacuated; but no sooner was all danger from that quarter at an end than Louis XII repudiated the treaty, on the ground that La Trémouille had greatly exceeded his powers.

In spite of the failure of Maximilian's hopes, he and Henry seem to have parted on friendly terms. Indeed, the last event of the campaign had been the treaty of Lille (October 17, 1513), between the two sovereigns and Ferdinand, which stipulated for a triple attack on France in the summer. Maximilian was to maintain 10,000 troops on the French frontier in return for a substantial subsidy from Henry VIII, and Charles's betrothal to Mary of England was formally renewed. But the unscrupulous Ferdinand only signed this treaty to infringe it. Ere six weeks had elapsed, he had formed a close alliance with Louis XII, which was to be cemented by the marriage of the Princess Renée to one of Ferdinand's grandsons. Milan and Genoa were to form her dowry, and were to be jointly occupied by the two sovereigns until the marriage was actually accomplished. Although the execution of this treaty could not but thwart one at least of Maximilian's projects —the marriage of Charles and Mary, and that of young Ferdinand and Anne of Bohemia—the Emperor was none the less won over by the wiles of the Catholic king to listen to French proposals of peace. The earnest dissuasions and sagacious advice of Margaret fell upon deaf ears. "It seems to me", she wrote, "that this is done only to amuse you ... in order to gain time, just as happened last year by reason of the truce ... Small wonder if Ferdinand is the most readily disposed of you three towards peace; for he has what he wants". And again, "you know the great inveterate hatred which the French bear towards our House", and, "it is clear that now is the hour or never, when you will be able, with the aid of your allies, to get the mastery over our common enemies". Even her warnings that peace means that the Duchy of Burgundy will remain French and that Henry VIII, "if he sees himself deserted by you, will win for himself better terms than you will know how to secure", seem to have been entirely disregarded by the obstinate Maximilian. On March 13, 1514, the Emperor signed the treaty of Orleans with France, and so confident was he of Ferdinand's influence with his son-in-law Henry VIII, that he actually guaranteed the English king's adhesion. The natural result of such presumption was that Henry and Maximilian fell apart, and early in August the former made his own terms with Louis XII, fully justifying Margaret's prophecy that the French King would set more value upon a settlement with England than upon the less solid advantages to be gained from her father's goodwill.

Peace was followed in October by the marriage of the enfeebled Louis XII and the vivacious Mary of England, the rupture of whose betrothal to Charles completed the estrangement of Henry and Maximilian. But the gaieties and entertainments which heralded the new Queen's arrival proved fatal to the bridegroom. The death of Louis XII on New Year's Day 1515, and the accession of his cousin, the young and fiery Francis of Angouleme, produced a complete change in the political situation. The typical product of his age, the new sovereign personified only too well the France of the Renaissance and of the later Valois kings, combining all their exaggerated license and treachery with those debased ideals of chivalry which had replaced the ancient code of honour. His mind was fired by wild dreams of foreign conquest, and his accession was promptly followed by preparations for a fresh invasion of Italy. The treaties with England and Venice were renewed, and by the end of March the young Archduke Charles, who had assumed the Government in January, signed, at the instance of his tutor Chièvres, a treaty of peace and amity with France. But the French monarch was not to remain unopposed. A new league was speedily formed against him between the Pope, the Emperor, Ferdinand, Milan and the Swiss, the latter resolutely rejecting all Francis's overtures for peace. Undeterred by the threatening attitude of the League, Francis led a magnificent army of 60,000 men across the Alps, and in the desperate battle of Marignano (September 13 and 14, 1515) drove back the Swiss army by sheer hard fighting. Full 20,000 men were left dead upon the field, and the Swiss, exhausted by so crushing a defeat, were compelled to abandon the Milanese to yet another conqueror. Leo X promptly sued for peace, and the Spanish and Papal forces in North Italy were practically disbanded.

The strange inactivity and want of interest, which Maximilian would at first sight seem to have displayed, while such grave issues were at stake, must be attributed to an event of great importance in the history of his own dominions. This was no less than his reception, at Vienna, of the Kings of Hungary and Poland, which set a seal to the negotiations and labours of many years by a final understanding between the two dynasties. Under the terms of the Treaty of Vienna (July 22), Prince Louis of Hungary was definitely betrothed to Mary of Austria, while his sister Anne was delivered over to the Emperor to be educated, in view of her marriage with the young Archduke Ferdinand. The flattery and congratulations which surrounded these proceedings included the adoption of Louis by Maximilian as his successor in the Empire. But this was merely a formal move in the diplomatic game, calculated to win the support of the young Prince. The Emperor well knew that the Electors cared little for any wishes which he might express; otherwise we may be sure that Charles, not Louis, would have been designated. The completeness of Francis's success, and his efforts to rouse the Scots against England drove Henry VIII into the arms of Ferdinand (October 19). English gold was liberally expended among the Confederates; and in February, 1516, 17,000 Swiss mercenaries moved on Verona, to join the Imperialists. Maximilian, whose forces were further swelled by levies of Tyrol and the Swabian League, was thus enabled to take the offensive in North Italy, with better prospects of success than on any previous occasion. In March he led a well-appointed army of 30,000 men across theMincio, and forced the French and Venetians to raise the siege of Brescia and fall back upon their respective bases. Maximilian continued to advance rapidly beyond the Oglio and the Adda, until he was within nine miles of Milan itself. But now, when Bourbon was well-nigh incapable of any prolonged resistance, and when fortune, after so many rebuffs, seemed at length about to crown the Imperial arms with victory, Maximilian, for some inexplicable reason, hesitated to strike home, and withdrew his army once more behind the Adda. His motives for so extraordinary a step have never been discovered; and today we are as completely in the dark as were his own allies at the time. Pace, who, as English envoy in Maximilian's camp, had peculiar opportunities for clearing up the mystery, writes in his report to Wolsey, "that no man could, ne can, conject what thing moved him to be so slack at that time, when every man did see the victory in his hands, and the expulsion of the Frenchmen out of Italy". Maximilian's own version—that the difficulties of foraging, the enemy's superiority in cavalry, and the stoppage of English money necessitated a retreat—is, in the face of incontestable facts, most improbable; and the only plausible suggestion—that the Emperor's change of policy was produced by a liberal outlay of French gold—is pure conjecture, unsupported by proofs. If we may believe the testimony of Pace in a matter which concerned his own person (and there is no reason to suspect his honesty), the Emperor, in his straits for money, actually profited by the English envoy's helpless condition, to extort a large sum of money from him, declaring that in case of a refusal he would make terms with France and would inform Henry that Pace had been responsible for his defection.

The universal indignation which Maximilian's withdrawal aroused among the troops is shown by the nicknames of "Strohkönig" and "Apfelkönig" which werelevelled at him. The army rapidly melted away, and, after struggling through the Val Camonica in deep snow, he reached Innsbruck with but a few hundred Tyrolese troops. On May 26 Brescia surrendered to the French and Venetians, and of all the Emperor's conquests Verona alone continued its resistance.

The sorry outcome of Maximilian's last Italian expedition seriously impaired his credit, alike within the Empire and abroad. He now found it advisable to give heed to the counsellors of his grandson Charles, whose position had been materially altered by recent events. On January 23, 1516, the arch-intriguer Ferdinand had passed from the scene of his questionable triumphs; and the young Archduke was left master of the entire Spanish dominions, with all their boundless possibilities. In spite of Francis' intrigues in Gueldres and Navarre, and his scarcely veiled designs upon the throne of Naples, Charles persisted in a policy of friendship towards France. On August 13 he concluded the Treaty of Noyon, by which Francis was unquestionably the greater gainer. Charles' betrothal to the French king's infant daughter not only put in question his rights to Naples, but also condemned him to remain a bachelor for many years, until the bride should attain a marriageable age. He further undertook to win Maximilian's consent to the restoration of Verona to the Republic, for a sum of 200,000 ducats.

The Emperor at first repudiated an agreement which implied such a lowering of self-esteem, and again sought subsidies from Henry VIII. But the conclusion of the Perpetual Peace between Francis I and the Swiss (November 29, 1516) left him entirely unsupported, and revealed to him the hopelessness of further resistance. By a treaty at Brussels, Maximilian agreed to surrender Verona and to conclude a six months' truce with the enemy. But wounded pride still kept him from consenting to a permanent peace with Venice, and it was not till July 1518 that he finally acknowledged his discomfiture. A five years' truce was concluded, under the terms of which Maximilian retained Roveredo and the district known as "the four

Vicariates". But these small acquisitions were completely outbalanced by the extensive pledging of domains, tolls and other sources of revenues, which the long-drawn-out war had rendered necessary, and by the further accumulation of an enormous debt. The dream of restoring Imperial influence in Italy was thus finally and completely dissolved. While the French ruled supreme in the North of Italy and the Spaniards in the South, Germany alone saw herself excluded from the scenes of her former predominance. The blame of this failure must rest largely with the Imperial Diet, which hardly once throughout Maximilian's reign allowed itself to be moved by considerations of patriotism, and which by a studied neglect of the demands of foreign policy clearly thwarted the true interests of Germany. Yet, while there were several occasions on which the effective assistance of the Estates would have crowned the Imperial arms with success, it cannot be denied that on the whole Maximilian displayed an incapacity and want of decision which forms a striking contrast to his earlier record. The plain truth is that Maximilian lacked the distinguishing features of a great general, combining, if we may use a modern comparison, the qualities of a drill-sergeant and a cavalry-colonel. Brave as a lion himself, he was apt to forget the duties of a commander in the fierce delights of themelée; and the dashing successes of his tactics were often neutralized by the want of a connected plan for the whole campaign. But we cannot review his military failings without bestowing the highest praise on his organizing and disciplinary talents. The landsknechts, who spread the fame of the German arms throughout Europe, were mainly his creation. His eager care for their welfare, and his readiness to share their fatigues and privations, won him the entire devotion, nay adoration of his soldiers; and a personal bond of union was thus established between them, which accounts for their willingness to submit to a continual discipline, such as was still contrary to the practice of the age. Among his many other accomplishments he possessed a practical knowledge of the founder's trade, which enabled him to invent several kinds of siege -and field-pieces, and to introduce various minor improvements in the art of war.

In the summer of 1518, while the settlement with Venice was still pending, Maximilian met the Estates of the Empire for the last time, at the Diet of Augsburg. His two main objects—the election of Charles as his successor, and a permanent military organization with a view to a crusade against the Turks,—met with little encouragement from the Estates, whose minds were filled with religious grievances and dreams of a national German Church. Hence they were scarcely likely to assist the Emperor, when they realized that his present policy involved entire dependence upon the Pope. The endless complaints and proposals which characterized the Diet, "showed clearly that the highest power in the Empire no longer fulfilled its office, but also that the possibility of doing so had been removed from its hands". But Maximilian's comparative lifelessness at this time admits of another explanation, apart from his preoccupation with the Venetian Treaty. Throughout the year he had been in failing health, and the pathetic words in which he bade farewell to his beloved Augsburg suggest that he was conscious of his approaching end. "God's blessing rest with thee, dear Augsburg, and with all upright citizens of thine! Many a happy mood have we enjoyed within thy walls; now we shall never see thee more!". Possibly at the prompting of Cajetan, the Papal Legate, Maximilian gave a most pointed proof of his lack of sympathy with Luther, by leaving the city only two days before the monk arrived.

The closing months of his life were troubled by the uncertainty of the succession to the Empire. His efforts to secure Charles' election as King of the Romans had almost been crowned with success. The day before he left Augsburg, he induced four of the Electors to meet him and to give their consent to the scheme. But his hopes were dashed to the ground by the opposition of Frederick of Saxony and Richard von Greifenklau, Elector of Trier, who contended that no election for the crown of the Romans was possible, while Maximilian himself still remained uncrowned as Emperor, and that Charles, as King of Naples, was expressly debarred from the Imperial dignity. The cup of his disappointment was full, and the Emperor retired wearily to Innsbruck, hoping to end his days in peace beneath the shadow of his beloved Alps. But one final indignity awaited him. The burghers of Innsbruck, who had suffered severely on former occasions from the Emperor's insolvency, resolutely closed their gates upon him; and he was obliged to retire to Lower Austria. On January 12, 1519, Maximilian's adventurous career closed at the little town of Wels, not far from Linz. The body was interred without pomp in the Church of St. George at Wiener Neustadt; but his heart was removed to Bruges and buried beside the remains of the consort, whose early loss had robbed him of life's brightest joy. Thus, amid disillusionment and humiliation, ends the career which had opened so full of rich promise. With Maximilian passed away the last Holy Roman Emperor, in the true mediaeval sense. The dominion of Charles V was doubtless more universal than any which Europe had seen since the days of Charles the Great, but its universality was essentially modern rather than mediaeval—dynastic and personal, not founded on the old dreams of an united Christian commonwealth. "Henceforth the Holy Roman Empire is lost in the German, and after a few faint attempts to resuscitate old-fashioned claims nothing remains to indicate its origin save a sounding title and a precedence among the States of Europe"

IV

" The essence of Humanism is the belief . . . that nothing which has ever interested living men and women can wholly lose its vitality."—Walter Pater.

IT is with a certain sense of relief that we pass from the tragi-comedy of Maximilian's political life to those realms where lies his real claim to fame and gratitude. Great ambitions thwarted by the sordid details of poverty are never a pleasant subject of contemplation; and there have been few monarchs in whose lives they have played a more prominent part. But it may fairly be argued that all the more credit is due to one who, under such unfavourable circumstances, ever remained buoyant and full of the joy of living, and whose frequent disappointments never soured his enthusiasms nor turned him from the path of knowledge. The first of his race to welcome the new culture, and possessed of that joyous temperament which seems to offer immortal youth, Maximilian was acclaimed by the scholars of his day as the ideal Emperor of Dante's or Petrarch's dreams. His predecessors had shown little interest in intellectual pursuits. Sigismund had indeed crowned several poets, but was always too needy himself to spare much money for their salaries; Frederick III was devoid of literary tastes, and, in spite of his connection with Aeneas Sylvius, gave but slight encouragement to art or learning. But Maximilian surrendered himself, with all his habitual energy and enthusiasm, to the new spirit of the age.

In spite of his many political failures he remains to all time the darling of the scholar and the poet. This almost universal favour he did not win by liberal donations or the grant of lucrative posts, for he was seldom free from money embarrassments—nor by the maintenance of a gorgeous court and imposing ceremonial—for his endless projects and expeditions made any fixed residence impossible; but by his restless activity, his manly self-reliance, his wide and human sympathy with all ranks and classes of the people. Above all, he identified himself with the struggling ideals of a new German national feeling, and with the growing opposition to France, to Italy, and to Rome; and, as a national hero, inspired the devotion alike of the scholar, the knight, and the peasant. "Mein Ehr ist deutschEhr, und deutsch Ehr ist mein Ehr" is the ruling motive of his life; and the praise which is continually on all lips is, before all, the result of his passionate loyalty to that larger Germany of which the poet sings—

So weit die deutsche Zunge klingt

Und Gott im Himmel Lieder singt

Das soll es sein!

Das, wackrer Deutscher, nenne dein!

Nowhere is the general admiration more evident than in the Volkslieder and the popular poetry of the time. And even when death overtook him in the midst of complete failure and humiliation, no scornful voice is heard, and all is regret and loving appreciation.

First among earthly monarchs,
A fount of honour clear,
Sprung of a noble lineage,
Where shall we find his peer?
He stands a bright ensample
For other Princes' eyes.
The lieges all appraise him
The Noble and the Wise,
His justice is apportioned
To poor and rich the same.
Just before God Eternal
Shall ever be his name.
And God the Lord hath willed it,
Our pure, immortal King,
And welcomed him in glory,
Where ceaseless praises ring.
Our hero hath departed.
Time's sceptre laying down,
Since God hath, of His goodness,
Prepared a deathless crown.

A vital distinction is at once apparent between the Italian and the German Renaissance. In Italy the movement was essentially aristocratic and largely dependent upon the various Courts—the Medici, the Popes, the Dukes of Urbino. In Germany such open-handed patrons were few and far between. Albert of Mainz, Frederick of Saxony, and Eberhard of Würtemberg stand alone among the princes as patrons of learning; while Ulrich von Hutten is the sole representative of the Knightly order in the ranks of the Humanists. The political and intellectual development of the German towns is of great importance during this transition period, and it is in them that the leaders of the German Renaissance are to be found. The movement remained throughout municipal rather than aristocratic, making itself first felt where there was closest commercial intercourse with Italy—notably in the cities of Swabia and the Rhine valley. But for this very reason Humanism took deep root in the soul of the German people. Not merely aesthetic or sensuous, like the Italian movement, it had a profound ethical and national basis, on which the powerful art of Dürer, the sonorous language of Luther, the sweet singing of Hans Sachs, might safely rest. Almost from the very beginning it pursued a moral aim. It was inspired by no mere sordid quest of pleasure, but by a noble dream of purer manners and loftier ideals. It realized the decadence into which society, both lay and ecclesiastical, had fallen, and earnestly strove to arrest it in the only possible way— by the introduction of a new spirit at once into the details of daily life, and into the broad principles of national existence.

But as the Humanist movement gathered strength and influence, it remained isolated from politics and from those who ruled the destinies of the Empire, and, developing in various places and under separate leaders, tended to waste its energies through lack of systematic or united effort. Under such circumstances its unspoken appeal for assistance in high places met with an eager response from

Maximilian. For the last twenty-five years of his life he forms the central figure of the new movement— possibly not its most glorious or most brilliant representative, but yet giving life and uniformity to the whole. If for nought else, he would deserve to be remembered as the connecting link between the Humanists of Strasburg, Augsburg and Nuremberg.

In order to interpret this feature of the Emperor's character, we must present a slight sketch of the German Renaissance in its three main channels, with especial regard to Maximilian and his connection with the leading Humanists, and must then proceed to examine Maximilian's own literary achievements, and his relations to Science and Art in its various branches.

In a quaint old comedy written at the close of the fifteenth century, Cicero and Caesar are brought to life and taken round the cities of Germany. They are made to describe Strasburg as "the most beautiful of the German towns, a treasure and ornament of the Fatherland"; of Augsburg they exclaim, "Rome with its Quiriteshas wandered here"; while Nuremberg is pictured as "the Corinth of Germany, if one looks at the wonderful works of the artist; yet if you look at its walls and bastions, no Mummius would conquer it so easily". Such are the three great centresof the German Renaissance.

In Strasburg, education was the most crying need of the time; for though there were excellent schools in the Franciscan and Dominican convents, these were reserved for novices, the laity being wholly excluded. Jacob Wimpheling, under whom Humanism first took deep root in the city, was himself a pupil of the Deventer School, and, like them, devoted his energies to educational reform. His hopes of founding a University were not realized, and he had to content himself with forming the centre of a literary society, such as was formed both at Mainz and Vienna by Conrad Celtes. Wimpheling and his friends differ largely from their contemporaries in other parts of Germany. They were characterized by a theological bias which led them into violent and unprofitable controversies. Though himself a cleric, and thus a supporter of the spiritual order and ot orthodox belief, he indulged in fierce attacks upon the monks for their immorality, and in spite of his admiration for heathen authors, he pushed his defence of theology so far as to condemn the Art of Poetry as useless and unworthy to be called a science, and only to exempt from utter damnation the sacred poets of Christianity. He was equally limited in his patriotic polemics. His praise of everything German is only surpassed by his hatred for the French and Italians, his profound contempt for the Swiss. His best-known work, entitled *Germania*, was written with the double object of proving the exclusively German origin of Alsace, and of "defending the King of the Romans against the monks and secular preachers who attack him". Even the ingenuous arguments in which the book abounds, and the quaint array of authorities, from Caesar and Tacitus to Aeneas Sylvius and Sabellico, cannot blind us to the genuine patriotism, which is latent in every page.

"We are Germans, not French", he exclaims, "and our land must be called Germany, not France, because Germans live in it. This fact has been acknowledged by the Romans. For when they had conquered us, the Alemanni on the Rhine, and, crossing the river, saw that the dwellers on the further bank were like us in courage, stature, and fair hair, as well as in customs and way of life, they called us Germans, that is, brothers. But it is certain that we, these Germans, are like the realGauls neither in speech and appearance, nor in character and institutions. Hence our city and all Alsace is right in preserving the freedom of the Roman Empire, and will maintain it also in the future, in spite of all French attempts to win over or conquer us".

Such fervent expressions of German feeling must have called Maximilian's attention to Wimpheling, even without his vigorous defence of the Imperial dignity. In 1510, when Maximilian was opposed to Julius II, and hoped to intimidate him by recounting the wrongs of the German nation, he could think of none more versed in them than Wimpheling, and therefore requested him to draw up a summary of the French Pragmatic Sanction, such as would suit the needs of Germany. In March, 1511, he wrote to Wimpheling that he was about to hold an assembly at Koln, to deliberate with the French envoys as to summoning a general Council; and he begged him to think out means of redressing the various abuses, "without touching religion."

As a result of this request, Wimpheling drew up his *Gravamina GermanicaeNationis* and added the desired *Remedia*. But the Emperor's policy had already changed, and Wimpheling was informed through the Imperial Councillors that the moment was unfavourable for publication. Indeed, his labours only received the attention which they deserved, when they were employed as the basis of "The Hundred Grievances of the German Nation" (1522).

Side by side with Wimpheling stands Sebastian Brant, whose literary worth has probably obtained wider recognition than that of any German Humanist, with the sole exception of Erasmus. His *Narrenschiff* ("The Ship of

Fools") is penetrated by a deep religious spirit, and fearlessly attacks all the corruptions and abuses of the day, "branding as fools all those who are willing, for things transitory, to barter things eternal". Brant is in no sense a great poet; his verses are often stiff and ill-proportioned, and his matter frequently sinks to the level of the commonplace. But the appearance of "The Ship of Fools" caused an unparalleled stir, not merely in the republic of letters, but throughout the whole German people; and it owes its extraordinary popularity to its skilful intermixture of problems which were in all men's minds. He was the first to give full expression to the ideas of the middle classes (anticipating the manly independence of the Scottish poet) when he sang—

Aber wer hatt' kein Tugend nit,
Kein Zucht, Scham, Ehr, noch gute Sitt,
Den halt' ich alles Adels leer,
Wenn auch ein Fürst sein Vater wär'.

But the ruling motives which inspire his muse are the maintenance of the Church in her pristine purity, and the defence of Christendom against the onslaught of the infidel. While he preaches earnestly the Headship of Christ, and exhorts all men to put their trust in God rather than in mortal men, he is also never tired of enjoining reverence for the Emperor, and urging them to unite in loyal obedience to his wishes and aspirations. Apparently unconscious of his inconsequence, he upheld the principle of absolute Papal domination, and yet early associated himself with that august dream of the Middle Ages—the universal monarchy of the Emperor. For him he claimed the same power in the temporal, as the Pope exercised in the spiritual world. As the Pope was the organ of religion, so was the Emperor the source of Law; and the revival of his power as temporal head of Christendom was to coincide with the re-establishment of that order and discipline whose absence Brant so frequently laments. The whole fabric of these vast aspirations Brant rested upon Maximilian. He could not foresee that this prince, so brilliant, so chivalrous, so sympathetic, would disappoint the rich promise of his youth and fail to restore the fallen grandeur of the Empire owing to his schemes of family aggrandisement. He greeted his election with adulatory verses, protesting that under such a prince the Golden Age could not fail to return. The news of Maximilian's imprisonment at Bruges rouses a very whirlwind of indignant phrases, contrary to the whole spirit of his later teaching. "Destroy the Flemings", he cries, "extirpate the very race of this crime, hang and behead the miscreants, overturn their walls, and make the plough pass over this accursed soil. Such is the demand of justice". His belief in omens and portents is unlimited, and they are generally connected with Maximilian in some quaint and highsoundingverses. Thus the killing of an enormous deer on some hunting expedition inspires Brant with an absurd and laboured comparison. "No animal is nobler than the stag : thou, Maximilian, art the most noble of Princes. He stops astonished before things which seem new; thou also dost admire things new and great. At the approach of danger he pricks up his ear and places his young in safety; thou hearest the menacing noises of thine enemies, and dost protect thy people". A number of falcons which were seen to assemble and fly southwards is acclaimed as a symbol of Maximilian, aided by the Princes in his Italian expedition. "Destiny calls you, O Germans; go and restore the Empire in Italy". Even when it became evident that Maximilian was not destined to realize the poet's high ideals, such extravagances did not cease. Moreover, he was sustained by a personal attachment for the Emperor, which was deepened by his various visits to the Court and closer acquaintance with his early hero, and doubtless strengthened by the Imperialfavours bestowed upon him. And thus it is with unfeigned grief that Brant celebrates his death -

"O magnanimous Caesar, that hope is vanished which we had founded on thee while thou didst hold the sceptre. How should I restrain my tears? Thou wert worthy to live, thou the sole anchor of safety for the German nation. One swift hour hath removed thee : thou art no more, and misfortune assails the Empire".

Our subject is Maximilian, not Brant, and we may not linger. But the epitaph on the Strasburg poet's tomb should not be omitted, even in the translation; for it gives us a sure clue to a character which was sweet and winning in spite of all its extravagances. « Toi qui regardes ce marbre, souhaite à Brant le ciel! »

If in Strasburg the movement assumed a theological and educational character, in Augsburg it was rather directed towards politics and the study of history. Alike from its geographical position and from its industrial and commercial importance, Augsburg was thrown into close relations with Italy and Italian thought; and enthusiasm for classical studies was early introduced by Sigismund Gossembrot, one of the leading merchants of the city. The direction of the movement was further influenced by the Diets which were held within the city, and by the frequent visits of the Emperor Maximilian.

The place of Gossembrot was worthily filled by

ConradPeutinger, who returned from Italy in 1485, as a doctor of law,embued with all the ardour of a scholar. He became a prominent official of his native city, and retained his position for many years from inclination rather than from necessity, betraying throughout his writings the sharp eye and critical knowledge of the practitioner. His first meeting with Maximilian probably took place at Augsburg in 1491, and from this time onwards he was continually employed by the Emperor in various positions of trust. As ambassador, secretary or orator, he visited many countries in Europe, and, besides ordering affairs of politics, was entrusted with the truly humanist task of presenting and answering formal addresses and greetings. While in his foreign relations he was eager to maintain the honour of the German name, heskilfully used his double position as Imperial Councillor and Town-official to smooth over differences between Maximilian and Augsburg, to the advantage of both parties.

The Emperor's love of Augsburg led him to purchase various houses within the walls, and the castle of Wellenburg in the neighbourhood. His action was far from welcome to the burghers, who did not wish this powerful citizen to acquire too much property in their midst; and they were only pacified by the assurances ofPeutinger that Maximilian would raise no fortifications round the castle. On the other hand, during his honourable mission to Hungary (1506), he obtained from the Emperor a substantial grant of privileges for his native city—notably the right de *non appellando*.

But Peutinger was Maximilian's confidant not merely in political affairs. Indeed, his employment in Imperial diplomacy directly arose from his intellectual and artistic relations with Maximilian, who sought the support of every scholar in his attempt to place the Fatherland in the forefront of Art and Science. In ItalyPeutinger had learned the value of old Roman inscriptions, and in 1505 he was encouraged by Maximilian to publish a collection of the inscriptions of German antiquity. The Emperor and the scholar kept up a correspondence on the subject of ancient coins, large consignments of which were sent to Augsburg, by order of the former, from every part of the Empire. During Peutinger's visit to Vienna in 1506 he was monopolized for three whole days for learned conversation, and received a new and more important commission from Maximilian. He was to examine the letters and documents of members of the House of Hapsburg, and to prepare a selection of them for publication; and with this object he was assigned a special apartment in the castle of Vienna, to which chronicles and histories were brought for his use from all quarters. Here he remained for almost three months, and the fruit of his labours was the *Kaiserbuch*, or Book of the Emperors, which was unfortunately never published and which is now extant only in a few fragments. During his labours for Maximilian he seems to have acquired a great number of valuable manuscripts; and had his literary projects been fully realized, we should have gained an astonishing contribution to the historiography of the sixteenth century. But apart from his own unfinished writings, he edited and published, with Maximilian's approval, various early historical works,—the chronicles of Paul the Deacon and of Ursperg being of especial value. Moreover, he was charged by the Emperor with a species of censorship, by virtue of which he prevented the appearance at Augsburg of a Swiss Chronicle, containing statements derogatory to the House of Hapsburg. In short, in almost every phase of the struggle of culture and civilization, which Maximilian so gallantly led, we find Peutinger intimately engaged as his friend and fellow-labourer; and with Beatus Rhenanus we may truly exclaim, "Our Conrad Peutinger is the immortal ornament, not merely of the town of Augsburg, but also of all Swabia!"

The activity of Augsburg was not confined to historical studies. The rising art of Germany had found here a worthy representative in Hans Holbein, who, though not strictly a Humanist himself, took the deepest interest in the movement. His attitude is clearly visible from his portraiture of Erasmus, More, and other leaders of the Renaissance, and from his illustrations to the Praise of Folly and the Dance of Death. But Holbein, though the greatest of the Augsburg School, was too much of a wanderer to be thrown into close contact with Maximilian. The latter none the less found capable artists to give expression to his own literary projects. HansBurgkmair, the most distinguished of their number, produced over one hundred illustrations of *Weisskunig*, seventy-seven for the Genealogy, which consists of portraits of Maximilian's ancestors, and close upon seventy for the *Triumphal Procession*, the main idea of which belongs to Durer. Leonhard Beck illustrated a book of *Austrian Saints*, and the greater part of the famous *Tenerdank*; whilstFreydal represented in his *Mummereien* the various tournays and festivities of which Maximilian was the central figure. All these woodcuts and engravings were executed under the supervision of Peutinger, who also directed the casting of figures for Maximilian's tomb at Innsbruck, and the making of armour and warlikeequipments for the Emperor's own person. Indeed, Maximilian put his Humanist friend to very strange uses; for among the manifold commissions of Peutinger we find the selection of tapestries from the Netherlands, inquiries after the inventor of a special kind of siege ladder, the building of hatching-houses for the Imperial falcons, and the establishment of an important cannon foundry. The climax is reached when Maximilian employs Peutinger's historical knowledge to obtain the names of a hundred women famous in history, after whom he may christen the latest additions to his artillery!

Of the three centres of German Humanism, Nuremberg is the greatest and the most fascinating. The home of invention as well as of industry, it made no mere empty boast in the proverb, "Nürnberg Tand geht durch alle Land". Its churches and public buildings were the glory of the age, its craftsmen and designers perhaps then unequalled in the world. Its literary circle contains a larger number of distinguished names than any of its rivals. Meisterlin, the author of the famous Nuremberg chronicle, Cochlaus, the bitter satirist of Luther; Osiander, the celebrated Hebrew scholar and Reformed preacher; Jager the mathematician; above all Hans Sachs, the cobbler-poet, "the sweet singer of Nuremberg"—all these fill an honourable place in the annals of the city. But the central figures of its life are, beyond any doubt, Willibald Pirkheimer and Albrecht Dürer; in any case they would monopolise our attention on account of their intimate connection with Maximilian.

When still King of the Romans, he had resided at Nuremberg, and the joyous animation with which he entered into the life of the city won for him wide popularity. "When about to depart, we are told he invited twenty great ladies to dinner; after dinner, when they were all in a good humour, the Markgrave Frederick asked

Maximilian in the name of the ladies to stay a little longer and to dance with them. They had taken away his boots and spurs, so that he had no choice. Then the whole company adjourned to the Council House, several other young ladies were invited, and Maximilian stayed dancing all through the afternoon and night, and arrived a day late atNeumarkt, where the Count Palatine had been expecting him all the preceding day". As Emperor, Maximilian paid many visits to Nuremberg, and his first Diet was enlivened by a succession of brilliant masques, dances and tournaments, such as roused the enthusiasm of the local chroniclers. He remained on terms of great intimacy with Pirkheimer, who in many ways is the most typical figure of the German Renaissance. After an excellent education, at Padua and Pavia, in jurisprudence, literature and arts, Pirkheimerbecame councillor in Nuremberg, and won the special confidence of the Emperor both by his skilful diplomacy and by his patriotic assistance in the Swiss War. His great riches he employed not merely for the adornment of his own house, but also in generous support of less-favoured followers of the Muse. While he resembledPeutinger as diplomat, as historian, and as theologian, he had less of the temperament of a pedagogue, and more of the joyous nature of a true poet. As the representative of a great movement of the intellect, he was open to all its various methods and aspirations, and yet understood the lesson of self-restraint and concentration too well to exhaust his powers in a labyrinth of alternatives. With the true cheerfulness and humour of the man who knows the world, yet remains unsullied by contact with it, he and his friends devoted themselves to what is after all the highest philosophy, the study of mankind—hiding under a smiling face, nay, often a mocking mien, their confidence in the great destinies of the race. And yet a deep pathos attaches to Pirkheimer's closing days. Disappointed in his dreams of moral and spiritual regeneration for the people, he turned wearily back from the paths of the new doctrine to the bosom of Mother Church. His violent attack upon Johann Eck, his noble defence of Reuchlin, had seemed to foreshadow him as a leader of the Reformation. But his ideals were in reality of the past rather than of the future; and, brooding over his shattered hopes, he lingered out a solitary old age, whose sadness is but deepened by his swanlike lament for Dürer.

Dürer was indeed well worthy of all the praise which has been lavished upon him; for from all his works there shines forth the noble modesty of a pure good man. Though scarcely a scholar himself, his deep sympathy with the great movement is manifest not only in the manner in which his art interprets it, but also in his own written words. His letters to Pirkheimer from Venice form delightful reading and show the keenness of his sympathy and observation. The years which followed his return to Nuremberg, 1507-1514, were the most productive period of his life, as well as the period of his most intimate connexion with Maximilian. From them date the ambitious designs of the "Triumphal Arch", which, though executed under Maximilian's direct supervision, were entirely the idea of Dürer. No less than ninety-two large woodcuts, the production of which occupied Durer for two years, go to make up this imposing metaphorical picture. A structure in itself impossible is overburdened by portraits of all the ancestors of Maximilian, mythical as well as real, and by the many exploits and adventures of the Emperor's own life. But the work must be estimated less by the quaintness of its composition than by its sterling artistic qualities and by the important place which it holds in the development of German Art. The idea was further developed in the *Triumphzug* and the *Triumphwagen*, which was completed in 15 16. The Imperial and other triumphal cars were drawn by Dürer in sixty-three woodcuts, while the remaining seventy-four were prepared in Augsburg by HansBurgkmair and L. Beck. The procession, whose magnificence was to idealize Maximilian as the greatest of Princes, includes sketches of almost everything that ever roused the Emperor's interest. Landsknechts, cannon, huntsmen, mummers, dancers of every rank and variety, the noble ladies of the Court, are mingled with allegories of every Imperial and human virtue, elaborately grouped upon triumphal cars. The keen personal interest of Maximilian in the progress of the work is well attested. Indeed, he showed his impatience, while the various blocks were in progress, by frequently visiting not merely Dürer himself, but also the*formschneider* or blockcutter, who lived in a street approached by theFrauengasslein. Hence the old Nuremberg proverb, "The Emperor still often drives to Petticoat Lane".

Dürer was appointed painter to Maximilian, with a grant of arms and a salary of 100 florins a year; and a letter of the Emperor to the Town Council of Nuremberg is still extant, in which he demands Dürer's exemption from "communal imposts, and all other contributions in money, in testimony of our friendship for him, and for the sake of the marvellous art of which it is but just that he should freely benefit. We trust that you will not refuse the demand we now make of you, because it is proper, as far as possible, to encourage the arts he cultivates and so largely develops among you". These earnest words of Maximilian reveal to us very clearly his attitude towards the great movement of his day.

Yet, sad as it is to relate, Dürer never received payment for the ninety-two sheets of the "Triumphal Arch", which had cost him so much time and labour, and after Maximilian's death they were sold separately. But the Emperor may fairly be absolved from the charge of mean treatment of Dürer, for his own needs were great and many, and it is strictly true that he spent very little upon himself. The great artist was always treated with distinction as a personal friend of the Emperor, who, besides granting him a fixed salary, gave him material assistance in checking the forging and pirating of his engravings. He sometimes resided at Court, when Maximilian held it at Augsburg, and often employed his time in making sketches in chalk of the illustrious persons whom he met. On one occasion Maximilian was attempting to draw a design for Dürer, but kept breaking the charcoal in doing so. When the artist took the pencil and, without once breaking it, easily completed the sketch, the Emperor expressed his surprise and probably showed his annoyance. But Dürer was ready with his compliment. "I should not like your Majesty," he said, "to be able to draw as well as I. It is my province to draw and yours to rule".

Not the least interesting and important of Durer's commissions was to paint that portrait of the Emperor which now hangs in the Imperial Gallery at Vienna. The prominent nose, the hanging eyelid, the half-contemptuous, half-mournful turn of the lips, the wrinkled cheeks and neck, the long hair falling over the ears, the pointed bonnet with its clasp, the sombre flowing robes, form a striking picture and suggest a speaking likeness.

Disappointment, but also that peculiar attribute of the Hapsburgs, resignation, are clearly marked upon Maximilian's face. In the other two portraits by Dürer—a chalk drawing executed at the Diet of Augsburg (15 18) and a woodcut completed shortly before his death—the features are less rugged, and reveal somewhat more of the sanguine spirit of Maximilian's early days. With the exception of these sketches, Dürer's last commission for Maximilian was the exquisite decoration for the latter' s private *Gebetbuch* (Book of Prayer), of which only ten copies were printed, and which will ever remain one of the gems of artistic and devotional literature. With Durer's career after 1519 we are not concerned; but it is worthy of notice that his most brilliant work dates from the reign of Maximilian, and that his sympathy with "the nightingale of Wittenberg" seems to have partially diverted his attention from his art.

It must not be supposed that Maximilian's humanistic enthusiasms were confined to the three great centres which have just been described, or that he only helped on such movements as were already animated by a vigorous existence and a fair prospect of success. His own hereditary dominions were even more directly indebted to his efforts than were other parts of the Empire.

During the first century of its existence, Vienna University was an autonomous ecclesiastical corporation, over which the methods of the mediaeval Schoolmen held complete sway. But during the long reign of Frederick III, several circumstances combined to cast a blight upon its hitherto flourishing condition. During the Council of Basel it assumed a hostile attitude to the Pope, and its surrender of that position only emphasised its folly; while in the struggle of Frederick and his brother Albert the professors were unwise enough to dabble in politics and thus to throw off the immunity which guarded their proper sphere. Their open sympathy with Albert was fatal to a good understanding with Frederick, who never showed any favour to their body. Vienna further suffered from a six months' siege by Matthias of Hungary (1477) and from a violent outbreak of the plague (1481); and this had scarce abated, when war was renewed and Matthias overran the whole of Lower Austria. During the ensuing siege (December 1484 to June 1485) all lectures were inevitably suspended, and the whole work of the University was at a standstill. The refusal of the University authorities to take the oath of allegiance to Matthias—on the ground that, as a clerical corporation, they were independent of the temporal power — induced the conqueror to stop all the revenues which they derived from the government; and though he at length granted a sum sufficient for the payment of the Professors and other necessities, yet he never extended to Vienna the same liberality towards Art and Science which had distinguished his relations with Buda-Pest. By the time of his death (1490) Vienna University was in a state of almost complete decay.

Under such circumstances the recovery of Austria by Maximilian was greeted with joy on the part of the authorities, and immediate steps were taken to restore the tottering fabric of the University. Maximilian set himself definitely to transform it from a clerical corporation to a home of the new Humanism, and was aided in this difficult task by the Superintendent Perger, the intention of whose office was not only to control the Government grants, but also to decide upon their expenditure, and to refer to the Emperor all questions of professorial appointments.

In spite of much internal opposition, the Humanists ere long acquired predominance in the philosophical Faculty, the medicals threw off the monstrous requirements of Scholasticism, and the jurists began to study Roman as well as ecclesiastical law. The revival of Vienna soon roused the interest of that peculiar product of the Renaissance period, the wandering scholar. The first to visit the University was Johann Spiesshaimer—more celebrated as Cuspinian—who rapidly won favour with the Hapsburgs by a poem in praise of St. Leopold, Markgrave of Austria, and who was crowned poet by Maximilian shortly after his father's death, in presence of a brilliant and representative assembly. Soon afterwards he began to hold regular lectures on poetry and rhetoric, discussing such writers as Cicero, Sallust, Horace, Virgil and Lucan. But Perger's preference lay decidedly with the Humanists of Italy, many of whom he had known personally during his residence at Padua and Bologna. At his recommendation, Maximilian in 1493 summoned Hieronymus Balbus from Venice to Vienna, and appointed him lecturer on the Roman Poets. But the Italian's fiery temper soon led him into disputes with the University authorities, and after an unsatisfactory career of two years he found a fresh outbreak of plague in the city a convenient pretext for returning to Italy.Krachenberger and Fuchsmagen, the two councillors whom Maximilian had appointed to assist Perger, doubtless influenced by the unseemly brawling ofBalbus, were loud in their complaints of Perger's favouritism, and urged their Imperial master to encourage German rather than Italian scholars. But Maximilian was, after all, only following his own judgment, when in 1497 he sent a cordial invitation to Stabius and Celtes to fill professorships at Vienna.

Conrad Celtes is the most famous of the earlier German Humanists, and is in a sense the forerunner of Peutinger andPirkheimer. But while his influence penetrated into every part of the Empire as a stimulating force, Vienna was the scene of his longest and most definite labours, and hence all mention of him has been postponed till now. Born in 1459, in humble circumstances, Celtes devoted himself from youth to the pursuit of learning, studying the Roman classics in the leading universities of Germany.

Without any settled abode, he wandered from one university to another, associating with scholars and supporting himself by lectures on the philosophy of Plato, the rhetoric of Cicero, or the poetry of Horace.

In 1486 he visited Italy and made the acquaintance of all the famous Humanists of the age. On his return, the publication of his first treatise, the *Ars Versificandi*, brought him to the notice of Frederick III, by whom he was crowned as poet at the Diet of Nuremberg (1487). During the next four years he visited Cracow, Prague, Buda, Heidelberg and Mainz, and again settled down at Nuremberg in 1491. Here he published a life of St. Sebald, patron of the city, in Sapphics, and a treatise upon the origin and customs of Nuremberg itself. But within a year he was summoned to Ingolstadt as Professor of Poetry and Rhetoric, and here he was residing when Maximilian's letter reached him. The Emperor's appeal was not in vain, and Celtes took up his permanent abode in Vienna University in 1497, as professor of the same subjects as at Ingolstadt. His opening lectures, which treated the philosophy of Plato inconnexion with the Neo-Platonism of the Italian scholars, were regarded with suspicion and dislike by many members of the University; but his position was strengthened by the hearty support of Maximilian, who in 1501 appointedCuspinian, the intimate friend of Celtes, to the post of Superintendent. Celtes, and with him the Emperor, was convinced that new methods of instruction were necessary, if Humanism was to triumph over Scholasticism. A new institute was required, which should serve for the preparation and training of Humanism, a sort of seminary of Humanist scholars, not outside, but inside, the University.

These views led, in October 1501, to the foundation of the "CollegiumPoetarum et Mathematicorum" by Maximilian. Planned by Celtes with the active approval of Cuspinian, the College in no way formed a fifth Faculty, though it was directly connected with the Faculty of Arts. Of its two divisions, the first was devoted to the study of mathematics, physics and astronomy, the second to that of poetry and rhetoric. The right of the coronation of poets, which had hitherto lain with the Emperor alone, was now vested by Maximilian in Celtes, as director of his own creation. The most distinguished scholars were to receive the crown of laurel, as a mark of high distinction and as an incentive to further efforts. But this privilege was exercised by Celtes for the first and last time, when in 1502 he crowned Stabius, his former colleague at Ingolstadt, and now Professor of Mathematics and Astronomy at Vienna. All subsequent coronations of poets were by Maximilian himself; and the College of Poets fell into disuse after the death ofCeltes in 1508. Even had worthy successors to Celtes and Stabius been found, it is doubtful whether the College would have had a permanent existence. Its hybrid position, as an independent institution and yet an integral part of the University, was a source of endless bickerings and quarrels, which can scarcely have been a recommendation to foreign scholars.

Celtes' other peculiar institution, the "Literary Society of the Danube", which he had originally founded at Buda, and which transplanted itself to Vienna when he settled there, was a kind of academy or free union of scholars for the spread of Humanism. Its members were recruited from almost every nation, and were only held together by the personal influence of Celtes; on his death it shared the same fate as the College of Poets.

An interesting development of such Humanist unions formed itself in the mind of Aldus Manutius, the famous Venetian printer. He longed for the establishment of an academy which should devote itself to the perfecting of printing and to the spread of the Greek language, and he entertained the further hope of converting it into an educational institute, which should form a point of scientific intercourse between Germany and Italy, under the direct initiative of the Emperor. But though he approached Maximilian on the subject, he obtained nothing but vague promises of assistance, whose fulfilment was thwarted by the Emperor's lack of resources.

Besides his general services to Humanism, Celtes earned the gratitude of Maximilian by his attention to historical studies. His sketch of Nuremberg contains a valuable description of its buildings and its trades, its climate and its inhabitants. His eager investigations resulted in the discovery of the comedies of the Saxon nun Hroswith, whose lax morality has been adduced as a proof of their fictitious character, and the works of Ligurinus, upon which he and his friends lectured at Vienna. At the moment of his death he was engaged upon important work for Maximilian. His projected history of the origin of the House of Hapsburg still remained very much in embryo; but his great work, *Germania Illustrata*, had assumed very real dimensions and would, if completed, have eclipsed even the famous Nuremberg Chronicle.

The place of Celtes was filled in Maximilian's estimation by Stabius and Cuspinian. The former, who had been crowned poet in 1502, was appointed Historiographer by the Emperor in 1508, and was virtually monopolized for historical research. Even during Maximilian's last illness Stabius was employed to read aloud volumes of Austrian history. But his achievements in the field of history are of trifling value, and are not to be compared to his works on geographical and mathematical subjects.

Cuspinian is much more worthy of consideration, especially as his relations with Maximilian drew him in the same direction as Peutinger. Already Rector of Vienna University in 1500, he was incessantly employed by the Emperor on embassies and in affairs of politics. In the course of five years he was engaged in no fewer than twenty-four missions to Hungary, and he took the leading part in the negotiations of 1507 and 15 15, which resulted in the double marriage between Austria and Bohemia-Hungary, and the close union of Maximilian with Uladislas (1515).

Notwithstanding his political activity, he found time for medical and historical pursuits, lectures and public addresses on Philosophy and Rhetoric, and elaborate discussions with his Humanist friends. Besides editing several of the later classical authors, he brought out the *Weltchronik* of Bishop Otto of Freisingen, and the same writer's *Warlike Deeds of Frederick Barbarossa*. His own productions include an account of the Congress of Princes at Vienna in 15 15, and a sketch of *The Origin, Religion and Tyranny of the Turks,* which naturally roused Imperial interest. All his most important works exhibit traces of his connexion with   Maximilian.
His *Commentarii de Romanorum Consulibus* are   probably   the

most profound and critical; but his history *De Caesaribus et Imperatoribus Romanorum*, which employed him between the years 1512 and 1522, undoubtedly possesses the most practical interest, since it furnishes us with many valuable details of Maximilian's life and character. His other work, *Austria*, contains a complete history of the country up till 1519, as well as a geographical and topographical description of its several provinces. Unhappily it was not published till 1553, and by that time the maps which were to have been included had disappeared.

Under Maximilian's auspices, the medical faculty of the University was improved to an equal extent with the others, and an ordinance was issued imposing the severest penalties, at the hands of the magistrates, on all foreign physicians whose incompetence was discovered. Again, the Emperor's passionate love of music led to a distinct revival in that noble science. A famous choirmaster of the day, Heinrich Isaak, who had spent twelve years in the service of Lorenzo the Magnificent, was induced to settle at Maximilian's Court, where his labours raised the Imperial Chapel to a high level of musical excellence. Amongst other really valuable compositions, his setting to the poem attributed to Maximilian, "Innsbruck, ich muss dich lassen", is well known at the present day. The Court organist, Paul Hofheimer, was likewise esteemed the glory of his profession, and was the forerunner of a school of brilliant organists scattered throughout Germany.

Though Maximilian knew well how to employ the activity of the scholar and the artist, and to stimulate the most varied aspirations of his time, there is one necessary limitation to our praise of his attitude. The buoyancy of his nature was to some extent due to a trait of vaingloriousness, which gave a rosy colouring to his own achievements, and prevented him from seeing himself as others saw him. Moreover, this airy self-conceit led him to lay by material, which should win from posterity a more comprehensive admission of his greatness than was accorded either by the bare facts of his political life or by the estimate of contemporaries; and thus he naturally emphasized the common idea of that period—that history was a relation of the warlike and peaceful exploits of the monarchs of the world. And yet he often rose above his own limitations. At one time he eagerly entertained the idea of a great Monumenten-Sammlung, or collection of authorities for mediaeval German history; while his encouragement of critical inquiry atoned for the incompleteness of his own conceptions. Still his literary productions are crowded with passages of fulsome adulation, which, by reason of over-statement and extravagant diction, rarely produce the effect intended.

Among these works two stand out prominently; yet even their execution was entrusted to others, partly no doubt on account of the many political demands upon Maximilian's time, but also because he did not himself possess sufficient patience or poetical talent. *Weisskunig* is a prose romance, much of the material of which was taken down from Maximilian's dictation by his secretaries, and re-arranged and compiled by MarxTreitzsauerwein of Innsbruck. It is divided into three parts, of which the latter is too obvious a mixture of "Wahrheit und Dichtung" to be of any great value. The earlier portion describes the life of the old White King (Frederick III), his journey to win his bride, his marriage and his coronation, while the second deals with the youth and education of the young White

King, Maximilian. The description of his endless accomplishments exhibits to the full the Emperor's love of minute information, as well as the happy conviction of his own excellence in almost every art and science. His quaint conversation with his father on the art of Government has already been referred to. Undoubtedly the chief interest and value of the book, which was only given to the world in 1775, lies in its illustrations, which show Maximilian engaged in the most varied pursuits. The charming picture of Mary and Maximilian teaching each other Flemish and German, the deathbed of Frederick III with its simple pathos, the humorous contrast of the young prince and his instructors in cannon-founding, his serious deportment over his correspondence—these are but four scenes chosen somewhat at random from a most fascinating collection.

Teuerdank, the other great prose-epic of Maximilian, is rather a fairy tale than a history, describing, under a highly allegorical form, the difficulties which opposed themselves to the Burgundian marriage. A fabulously wealthy King has an only daughter, a miracle of virtue and beauty, who is to belong to the most gallant and distinguished of her many suitors. King Romreich dies before a decision has been come to, but Princess Ehrenreich sees from his will that only Ritter Teuerdank is worthy of her hand. She summons him and he promptly sets forth to join her, accompanied by his trusty comrade Erenhold. But he is continually detained and led astray by the Evil One, who urges him to follow his natural instincts, and throws every kind of adventure in his way. Moreover, the envious magnates ofEhrenreich's Court enlist against him three captains, who endeavour to lure him to destruction. Fürwittig represents the vain ambition of youth, to give proof of its strength and skill and glory, merely for its own gratification; Unfalo, the fascination for the noble youth, which lies in travel and adventure by sea and land; whileNeidelhard personifies the deadliest of unseen enemies. Jealousy, that foe who leads the young Prince into the most difficult entanglements. But the gallantTeuerdank comes scathless through every ordeal, thanks to his innate virtue and to the powerful genius of Love. But even then his trial is not at an end. At the request of Ehrenreich, and the exhortation of a heavenly messenger, he conducts a campaign against the infidels, who consent to become his vassals. At length he is free to return, covered with glory and honour, to the Court of Ehrenreich, when the marriage is duly celebrated. This extravagant romance, which, with all its sentiment, is inclined to be wooden and tedious, was actually composed by Melchior Pfinzing, Provost of St. Sebald's, Nuremberg, though Maximilian directed its whole tone and substance. It also was elaborately illustrated by Beck,Burgkmair, and others, but its woodcuts are much inferior in interest and in execution to those of *Weisskunig*.

In 1517 the whole work was privately printed upon parchment, but in 1535 it was published to the world in an edition which is famous for its sumptuous style. The *Ehrenpforte* and *Trimnphzug*, the *Genealogie* and *Wappenbuch* lend additional force to the argument that Maximilian's enthusiasm owed part of its vigour to motives of self-glorification. The most important of these works have already been referred to in connection with the Augsburg artists and with Dürer. But some mention must here be made of the recently discovered *Gejaid Buck*, which was written for Maximilian during 1499-1500, by his Master of the Game, Carl vonSpaur, and adorned with rich illuminations, dealing with the Emperor's sport on the mountains of North Tyrol.

This book contains such minute information, that he could at a glance "ascertain the head of chamois and red deer in any of the 200 and odd localities described therein", and is full of hints and suggestions as to the posting of the sportsmen and as to possible quarters for the night. Often when there was no castle in the neighbourhood, the Emperor had to content himself with a primitive log-hut high up on the mountain-slopes. Sometimes, to avoid such rough lodging for the night, he covered tremendous distances on horseback, to get back to more frequented valleys; and it was doubtless on such an occasion as this that he found a beggar dying by the roadside, and, dismounting, gave him his own flask to drink from, wrapped his own mantle round him, and then rode hotly to the next town to summon a priest. Fatigue was well-nigh unknown to him, and he must sometimes "have started from his headquarters in the middle of the night, getting back only after some thirty-six hours in the saddle. . . . Only those acquainted with the very voluminous correspondence of this keen sportsman can form any idea of the close attention paid by him to every detail connected with the chase. ... In the thick of a bloody war in the Netherlands we find him writing letters about a young ibex buck some peasant women in a remote Tyrolese valley were keeping for him, or promising in an autograph letter a silk dress to each of certain peasants' wives in an isolated glen, as a reward for preventing their husbands from poaching this rare game, or giving minute instructions where a particular couple of hunting hounds were to be kept, and what was to be done with their puppies". Our astonishment is not lessened when we learn that Maximilian possessed as many as 1,500 hounds.

This brief digression, to which the Emperor's literary

works have inevitably tempted us, is far from inappropriate to any description of one whose passion for the chase led him to sign himself "sportsman and Emperor". Thus, in all their manifold branches, Literature, Art and Science owe Maximilian a deep debt of gratitude. He worthily led the great onward movement of his day, devoting himself to its cause with wholehearted service. He guided and controlled it up to the very threshold of that mighty Revolution, in which "a solitary monk" was destined to shake the world; and on the threshold it was but fitting that he should leave its direction to others. His little foibles and conceits vanish, in view of the great fact that he had nobly performed his duty in the march of time; and it would indeed have been a cruel mockery of fate, had he been left to see his ideals shattered and falsified, the world of his conception renovated and transformed, while he himself, too old in years and too passionate in conviction to remain leader of the van, dropped backward amid the indistinguishable throng.

Though Maximilian was wholly out of sympathy with the principles which guided Luther, and would probably have opposed him had he lived, yet it may be said that indirectly the Reformation owes something to him. The earlier stages of the German Renaissance were dominated by a strong theological bias, and it was only gradually that the prevailing idea was dispelled, that a student or literary man must belong to the spiritual order. The revival of the study of Greek and Hebrew strengthened the element of criticism; and with criticism of theology came criticism of history, and a desire to dispel the mists which had gathered round the great past of Germany, and to kindle the growing national spirit by a closer knowledge of the glorious deeds of men's ancestors. This patriotic movement, which no one did more to foster and encourage than Maximilian, soon brought the passionate upholders of Germany into collision with foreign sentiment. The opposition to Italy and to Rome, which was mainly due to the degradation of the Papacy and its practice of draining German resources for purely Italian ends, was regarded with favour by Maximilian, though his policy was possibly dictated by secular considerations. Wimpheling's attack on Papal abuses in Germany, written at Maximilian's command, is the most outspoken defiance of Rome prior to the appearance of Luther. But while Maximilian possessed that deep national enthusiasm which was one of the leading inspirations of Luther's career, he had none of the Reformer's profound criticism and self-depreciation, and was too much a man of action to take any deep interest in questions of theology.

We cannot pass to a final estimate of Maximilian's character and policy without some mention of the wonderful monument in the Hofkirche at Innsbruck. The Church itself was erected in compliance with the will of Maximilian, but owing to the loss of the original plans, the whole work was not completed till the year 1583. In the centre of the nave stands a massive marble sarcophagus, which supports the kneeling figure of Maximilian, surrounded by the four cardinal virtues. On the sides of the sarcophagus are twenty-four exquisite marble reliefs, representing the principal events of the Emperor's life, all but four of which were executed by Alexander Colins of Mechlin, the architect of the famous Otto-Heinrichsbau in Heidelberg Castle. Many of the reliefs are especially interesting for the careful studies of faces; those of Maximilian's meetings with his daughter Margaret and with Henry VIII contain striking portraits of the Emperor.

But the unique feature of this famous memorial is the long line of bronze figures which extend round the nave, the silent witnesses of the vanished grandeur of the Holy Roman Empire. All the great rulers of the House of Hapsburg here watch over what should have held the mortal remains of their gallant descendant; while the gentle Mary and her children take their places in the silent pageant. But amid all the throng two figures stand out conspicuously. Maximilian had wished that the heroes of his early dreams should share the long vigil over his grave; and the magic power of Peter Vischer, the great Nuremberg craftsman, has given the touch of life and genius to the figures of Theodoric and Arthur. Fitting indeed it was that the personality of the champion of the Table Round should be made to rise before us. Arthur, the great type of all that was best and noblest in mediaeval chivalry, and Maximilian, the last worthy representative of a worn-out order and a subverted code of honour, are thus indissolubly linked together in our imaginations; and as we turn away from the empty tomb and its spellbound watchers, we can realize something of the glamour and romance of the Imperial dreamer's life.

V

THE wideness of Maximilian's interests, and the variety of spheres in which those interests led him to take a part, enhance the difficulty of estimating or defining his character as a whole, and each different attitude demands discussion before any general conclusion can be drawn. His political career, however, despite all its intrigues and complications, is comparatively easy to estimate; for his persistence in controlling his own policy and his dislike of associates and confidants throw the entire responsibility of any given action upon the Emperor's own shoulders. His retentive memory and tireless energy aided him in what would otherwise have been a hopeless effort.

"He seldom or never", writes the Venetian ambassador in 1496, "discusses with any one what he has in hand or does, especially in important matters". He was in the habit of dictating to his secretaries late into the night, and often drew up important documents with his own hands; while even during his meals, and in the midst of his hunting expeditions, he dictated dispatches or gave instructions to hiscouncillors. For his credit as a politician this monopolizing spirit was most unfortunate. His secrecy kept his councillors and ambassadors ever in the dark, and rendered a firm attitude on their part almost impossible. His over-confidence, both in his own capacity and in the honesty of others, received many a rude shock, and often made him the dupe of his intellectual inferiors. Machiavelli tells us the opinion of an intimate friend of the Emperor, "that anyone could cheat him without his knowing it". His condemnation as a bungler by the Florentine statesman has been used as an argument in Maximilian's favour; but the only possible inference is that in affairs of state the Emperor's morals had not suffered so complete an eclipse as those of his rivals, while his statecraft was based upon a neglect of sound political principles.

But even more prominent than the self-centred nature of his policy are two fatal weaknesses in his character, which account for most of his failures and disappointments—his want of perseverance and his openhandedness.

The whole history of his reign is an illustration of the inconstancy with which he flitted from scheme to scheme, never allowing the time necessary for a successful issue; and the disastrous consequences of this habit were only accentuated by the fact that he remained a law unto himself, self-deprived of all moderating influences. It was this fickle and over-sanguine disposition which caused Louis XII to exclaim, "What this King says at night, he does not hold to the next morning". The criticism of Ferdinand V is perhaps even more apposite—"If Maximilian thinks of a thing, he also believes that it is already done". Without duly considering the means at his disposal, he stormed impetuously towards an end which was obviously unattainable under the circumstances, and, to make matters worse, he had already lost all interest in the project before there was even a prospect of its being crowned with success. In other cases, his inventive intellect showed him two or three ways towards the same goal, with the result that he either pursued all at once, or, confining himself to one only, soon changed his mind and adopted a course which he regarded as safer. "And so," writes Quirini, "he springs from one decision to another, till time and opportunity are past . . . and thus he wins from all men a light enough reputation."

But perhaps the greatest weakness of Maximilian's administration was faulty finance. It is true that the resources at his disposal were wholly inadequate, whether in the Empire or in his own dominions. Yet his own unpractical and visionary nature prevented him from making the best of such means as he possessed, and drew him into quite a needless amount of money difficulties. He had absolutely no conception of the meaning of economy, and, deeming it anunkingly trait, gave with both hands to his servants and his friends, and laid no proper check upon his household expenses. The fact that he spent but little upon himself, and that his personal requirements were frugal in the extreme, while it speaks well for the generosity of his nature, cannot affect our estimate of his financial incapacity. Indeed, such were his extravagance and his penury, that the Venetian ambassador was induced to exclaim : "For a ducat he can be won for anything". And truly, the fact that he actually served Venice and Milan, and in later years England, for hire, after the manner of an Italian condottiere, justifies the severe exaggeration of this remark. His liberal patronage of Art and Science, and the magnificence of the Court entertainments, must have contributed in some degree to his popularity among contemporaries; but his ruinous method of raising supplies in his own dominions really transferred the burden of his endless undertakings to the shoulders of the next generation.

As Emperor, Maximilian has been severely censured for subordinating the Imperial to the territorial ideal, and for furthering Hapsburg ambitions at the expense of Germany as a whole. But a survey of his youth and early training at once helps to explain this policy and proves it to have been inevitable. Such a path had been mapped out for him by his father's motto, A.E.I.O.U., and Frederick's own impotence to achieve its aspirations only served to impress it more firmly upon the youthful Maximilian. And indeed there is much truth in his idea, that the building up of a strong hereditary State was the surest road towards an imposing position in the Empire. While the personal defects of Maximilian, which have already been discussed, are largely responsible for the comparative ineffectiveness of his Imperial policy, yet the chief cause of all was inherent in the constitution of the Empire. It can hardly be doubted but that an Emperor far more powerful than Maximilian ever was would have failed to combine the many conflicting elements into a central Government capable of strong and united action.

"Constitution, Law, order in the State were everywhere forcing themselves out of the perverted forms of the Middle Ages into more perfect models." But as yet confusion and impotence held sway, and the broad principles of reform were obscured from Maximilian's eyes by a perplexing array of minor questions. Feudalism had long been in decay, and the efforts of rulers in every State were directed towards extending their authority and bringing the nobles and the towns into greater dependence upon the throne. But the permanent taxation and the standing army which made the attainment of this end possible to the French kings, and through which France became for a number of years the first military power of

Europe, were denied to Maximilian by the peculiar circumstances of the Empire. Not even in his hereditary lands, still less elsewhere, was there any regular system of "aids" for the sovereign's support; and Maximilian had to wage his wars, either with militia, who were ever slow to assemble and prompt to disband, whose discipline was not beyond reproach, and who were not liable to serve outside their own territory, or with mercenaries, whose maintenance involved an expense which the absence of regular taxation made it difficult to meet.

Apart from the revenues of Crown lands and the deeply mortgaged mines and tolls, he could raise no contributions without the Diet's consent; and as a rule each Estate vied with the others in resolutely setting aside all considerations of patriotism and maintaining the tightest hold upon their purse-strings. They showed no sympathy with Maximilian's aims and interests; while the Emperor lacked the power to enforce his wishes upon them. Such circumstances would almost justify his policy of retaliation by obstructing the Diet's efforts towards reform. But in any case he can hardly be blamed for falling back upon a strictly Austrian policy and using his Imperial office to further Hapsburg interests.

Whenever the Emperor's political action is deserving of praise, the House of Hapsburg rather than the Empire will be found to have reaped the benefit. His enthusiastic belief in the future greatness of his House was the guiding star of his whole life, and encouraged him to consolidate his dominions internally, and thus, as he hoped, to fit them to become the central point of a world-wide empire.

Besides the introduction of Roman law, for which he was mainly responsible, he thoroughly reorganized the administration of the Austrian Duchies. The revenues had become insufficient for the execution of his princely duties, especially in time of war; and Maximilian set himself to introduce into the country the same methods of Government which he employed in the Netherlands. He replaced the old feudal survivals in the State by a modern officialdom, which gradually paralyzed the opposition of the Estates, and from which certain individuals exercised a permanent control over the government during his own absence.

Meanwhile it was his Hapsburg and territorial ambitions which prompted him to reassert the Imperial authority in Italy, and which were partly responsible for his eagerness to recover Croatia and Southern Hungary from the hands of the Turks. Above all, it was these ambitions that inspired him in his endless projects of alliances and marriages—projects which secured for his descendants the glorious inheritance of Spain, the two Sicilies and the New World, and the Kingdoms of Bohemia and Hungary.

Passing from his public to his private life, we may reasonably assert that Maximilian, while far from spotless, compares favourably with the Princes of his time. The excesses of Charles VIII, the luxurious vice of Louis XII, the barbaric licentiousness of Francis I, and again the unrestrained passions of Henry VIII, and Ferdinand V's frank disavowal of morality—all these traits are happily wanting in Maximilian's life. He seems to have loved the gracious Mary faithfully and tenderly, and it is said that, to the day of his death, any mention of her name drew from him a deep sigh of remembrance. But for her untimely death he might have resisted the fierce temptations of his royal position. He had at least eight natural children, of whom two only are known to history—George, Bishop of Brixen, who eventually became Prince Bishop of Liege, and a daughter, who perished with her husband, the Count of Helfenstein, in the Peasants' Revolt of 1525.

It cannot be maintained that Maximilian's second marriage was a love-match; yet there is reason to believe that, though he paid little attention to the unfortunate Bianca Maria, he at least remained faithful to her.

Though his table was always magnificently served, he himself was extremely temperate, both in food and drink. Indeed, his strong detestation of drunkenness forms a pleasant contrast to the opinions and practice of his courtiers and even of the great princes of the Empire. His moderation and healthy diet gave added strength to a frame which was naturally robust and untiring. He could endure with ease the extremes of heat and cold, prolonged journeys and want of sleep, and even privations in food and drink. His strong constitution was united to a pleasing countenance, which seldom failed to prepossess in his favour. A prominent nose and well-defined features, together with the lightning glances of his eye, imparted to him a searching look, which seemed to pierce through men and read their very souls. Withal, he was fully endowed with that genial and gracious manner which veils its condescension under a mingling of good humour and perfect tactfulness. In conversation he exercised a fascination which was not without its effect even upon his sternest opponents; while the whole-hearted and friendly spirit with which he threw himself into the amusements and sports of the common people won for him an even wider respect and love than his passion for the chase and his intimate relations with the Tyrolese mountaineers. He frequently took his place in a village dance, or competed with the peasants in their shooting matches; and he recommended the chase to his descendants not merely for those delights which none knew better than himself, but also because of the opportunities which it offered to princes of coming into contact with their subjects, of learning their wishes and helping them in their difficulties. His fresh joyous nature showed itself in a thousand little touches, but perhaps in none more vividly than in his ardent love of music and in the delight which he took in the presence of singing birds in the palace of Innsbruck. Thus whether fraternizing with the peasants of his beloved Tyrol, clad in a hunting suit of simple grey, or affably conversing with the burghers and ladies of Frankfort or Augsburg, he awoke in all hearts an involuntary feeling of admiration.

Before all, Maximilian was a German of the Germans. As he was the last representative of the dying mediaeval chivalry, and the last monarch of the ancient German stamp, so also he was the first German patriot-king of modern times; and herein lies the secret of the love and admiration which his contemporaries poured so fully upon him. The proud and royal motto to which he gave utterance, "My honour is German honour, and German honour mine", graphically reminds us that he identified himself with the joys and sorrows, the glories and the failures of the German race. It is neglect of this fact, and want of sympathy with German thought and ideals, that are responsible for the indiscriminating criticisms of several modern historians—criticisms which would often be bestowed with greater justice upon the constitution of the Empire than upon the Emperor himself. And the motto has been realized in a further sense. For the feeling of Germany, turning from the weaknesses and failures which mar the fullness of Maximilian's glory, has reciprocated the loyalty which he expressed towards his people, and has elevated the chivalrous Emperor into one of the national heroes, worthy to rank with Hermann and Barbarossa. For Maximilian, in no uncertain sense, personified the dreams, the aspirations, the strugglings of the Fatherland. The nation, chastened and revivified by a new birth of patriotism, sought an object on whom to fix its affections and its hopes. It turned naturally to the Emperor, the heir of so many splendid traditions, and it was met on his side by the ardent devotion of a whole lifetime. In a word, he and his people had realized— incompletely it may be, yet in a very genuine sense—the true relations of a monarch and his subjects, and, linked to one another by ties of mutual sympathy, handed down the happy tradition as an example to their remote posterity. "Kaiser Max" (as his people fondly called him) was not a great man, in the strictest sense of the word; yet all lovers of large-hearted and human characters must ever treasure his memory in their hearts.

And here let us take our leave of Maximilian, in the kindly words of a contemporary—

Here upon earth small rest to thee was given,

Now God hath granted thee the joy of Heaven.

APPENDIX

THOUGH some reference to Maximilian's relations to the question of Imperial Reform was unavoidable, a detailed account must be sought for rather in an authoritative history of Germany than in an essay which centres round an individual. Hence an appendix seems the most fitting place for dealing with the subject.

When Maximilian was elected King of the Romans (1486), it had long been evident that, if a new or reformed constitution was to be secured, the initiative must be taken by the Estates. During the years 1486-89 frequent deliberations took place, with a view to evolving some scheme for strengthening the institutions of the Empire. The leaders of the movement sought especially to impart to the Imperial Diets more regular forms and greater dignity, and to check the resistance to their decrees which was met with in the towns. At the Diet of 1487, the towns, renouncing the policy of obstruction and equivocation which had characterized them throughout the century, were fully represented, and took an active part in the business of the committee which discussed the Landfriede. In 1489 a new stage of development was reached by the Diet, when the Tree Colleges of Electors, Princes and burghers separated for the first time and conducted their deliberations apart. Their proposal to limit the power of the Imperial Tribunal met with determined opposition from

Frederick the Third; and the Estates applied to Maximilian, and obtained from him a promise of the reform of the Kammergericht, or Imperial Chamber. The old Emperor's attitude necessitated a postponement of the question; but on his death in 1493 it was revived with greater urgency than ever. The leading spirit of the whole movement was Berthold of Henneberg, Elector of Mainz, whose patriotism and calm impartiality won the respect of all parties. At the great Diet of Worms, which opened at the end of March 1495, the Estates united in pressing on Maximilian a fulfilment of his promises, and persisted in refusing him all support until he submitted to their demands. The struggle lasted throughout the summer, Maximilian throwing every obstacle in the way of reform, but finally, on August 7, he signed his agreement to the demands of the Diet. The results of the Diet may be classified under four heads :

1st. The Landfriede was more closely organized, and was made perpetual. No difficulty was experienced over this point, as Maximilian had taken the lead in enforcing the Landfriede at an earlier date.

2nd. The Kammergericht, or Imperial Chamber, was founded, to act as a court of first instance for all direct subjects of the Emperor. Its jurisdiction was, however, limited to cases of prelates, nobles, knights and towns among each other; in the event of complaints against any of the princes or electors, an arbitration was first necessary before the councillors of the accused Prince. The Chamber consisted of a judge, nominated by the Emperor, and sixteen other members, appointed by the Estates, half being of knightly birth, half learned in the law.

Its distinguishing features were :

(a) That it was to sit continuously in the Empire, not following the court, but fixed permanently at Frankfurt-on-Main.

(b) That it could receive appeals from the Landgerichte.

(c) That its members were to receive their salaries out of the fees of the court, though they might be supplemented from the Imperial revenues if these fees proved insufficient.

(d) That the judge acquired the power of proclaiming the ban of the Empire in the sovereign's name.

3rd. A proposal was laid down for yearly meetings of the Estates, with the object of controlling the Imperial expenditure. To this assembly the treasurer was to deliver the money which he received from the taxes, and it was to hold the exclusive power of deciding the expenditure; while neither the Emperor nor his son might declare war without its consent.

The constitution thus proposed was a mixture of Monarchical and federal Government, but with an obvious preponderance of the latter element; a political union, preserving the forms of the ancient hierarchy of the Empire. But the defective nature of the Diet's composition, and the virtual impossibility of securing a united effort for any length of time, prevented the accomplishment of this scheme.

4th. In return for these concessions on the part of Maximilian, the Diet instituted "The Common Penny". This was an attempt at systematic taxation, according to which an impost of half a gulden was levied on every 500 gulden, and among the poorer classes every twenty-four people above the age of fifteen contributed one gulden.

The Common Penny was imperfectly organized and soon became merely nominal, as the needy Maximilian often found to his cost; and though it was revived under Charles V, it soon disappeared again after a brief and fitful existence.

The only actions of the Diet of Lindau (1496), the next in succession to that of Worms, were to renew the Common Penny, to transfer the Imperial Chamber from Frankfurt to Worms, and to impose a tax upon the Jews of the chief Imperial towns.

Though Maximilian had at Worms evaded the demand for a Reichs-regiment, or Council of Regency, as too serious a limitation to his prerogative, yet at the Diet of Augsburg (1500) he was obliged to give way even at this point. The Diet gave its sanction to a scheme of military organization, according to which every 400 inhabitants were to provide one foot soldier, the cavalry was to be raised by the Princes and nobles upon a fixed scale, and a tax was imposed on those who could not themselves take any active share. In return for this concession, Maximilian consented to the establishment of a Council of Regency, which, had it preserved the powers which were at first granted to it, would have deprived the Emperor of whatever power he still possessed. It was composed of a President, chosen by the Emperor, one delegate from each of the Electors, six from the Princes conjointly, two from Austria and the Netherlands, and two from the Imperial cities. Its powers were most comprehensive, and included the administration of justice, the maintenance of peace, the defence of the Empire from attack, and, most astounding of all, the control of foreign affairs. It is conceivable that

Maximilian might have submitted to the Council's authority, had it displayed becoming moderation. But its first act—the conclusion of peace with France—was so directly contrary to the whole trend of Maximilian's policy, that he was naturally driven into active opposition to its powers.

In 1502 he fell back upon his Imperial right of holding Courts of Justice (Hofgerichte) , and erected a standing court or Aulic Council (Hofrath), entirely under his own control. He himself was its president, and its assessors were arbitrarily appointed. This action led to a congress of Electors at Gelnhausen in June 1502, at which they arranged to meet four times a year to deliberate on public affairs, and actually announced the first meeting for the following November, without consulting the Emperor in any way upon the matter. Maximilian was too weak to oppose them, and therefore proclaimed the assembly himself. But the successful issue of the War of Landshut and the death of Berthold of Mainz greatly strengthened Maximilian's position in the Empire, and proportionately weakened the cause of Reform. Hence the Council of Regency was allowed to die a natural death.

At the Diet of Constance (1507) some progress was again made. In return for a grant of troops and money, Maximilian re-established the Imperial Chamber, which had held no sittings for three years, and a small tax was instituted to pay the salaries of its officials.

The Diets of Worms (1509) and Augsburg (1510) were occupied by complaints and abuse, which were wholly without effect. In 1512, however, the Diet of Koln, to which city it had removed from Trier, secured the division of the Empire into sixKreise, or Circles, for administrative and military purposes. The Circles were to be placed under

Captains, who were all controlled by a Captain-general, and the organization was to be entrusted to a council of eight, "who were to act as a Privy Council under the Emperor's control". But the jealousy of the Diet refused him the nomination of these Captains, and of the council, with the result that the measure fell through for the time, and did not take effect till 1521, under Charles V.

This was the last serious attempt at Reform during the reign of Maximilian; for the later Diets were mere scenes of confusion and of mutual recrimination. The failure of the reforming movement only served to emphasize the fact that the constitution of the Empire had become an unworkable machine, and that the Empire itself could only be saved from weakness and disorganization by the rise of a strong central monarchy. But this was not to be. Such a contingency, which Maximilian's vast dreams of Austrian world-power had seemed to foreshadow, was rendered impossible by the great spiritual revolution, which filled all minds throughout the reign of Charles V. Several centuries were required to permit the growth of a strong German state out of the chaos of the mediaeval Empire; and it was reserved for the nineteenth century to see a native dynasty restore to Germany the long-lost blessings of consolidation and unity.

Made in the USA
Las Vegas, NV
01 May 2022